FREE STUFF FOR TRAVELERS

FREE STUFF FOR TRAVELERS

The Free Stuff Editors

Director: Bruce Lansky
Editor: Tom Grady
Asst. Editors: Louise Delagran, Amy Rood

OUR PLEDGE

We have selected the best of all offers available. The suppliers have promised, in writing, to honor single-copy requests through June 1982 — and beyond, as long as supplies last. We will monitor the suppliers and keep the book updated and accurate. We're dedicated to making this a book that really works.

Meadowbrook Press

18318 Minnetonka Boulevard ● Deephaven, Minnesota 55391

First Printing March 1981

Design: Terry Dugan

Library of Congress Cataloging in Publication Data

Main entry under title:

Free stuff for travelers.

   Includes index.
   1. Travel—Catalogs. 2. Free materials—Catalogs.
I. Lansky, Bruce. II. Grady, Tom, 1951–
G151.F73   910'.2'02   81–2305
ISBN 0–915658–29–1   AACR2

Printed in the United States of America
ISBN 0-915658-29-1
© 1981 by Bruce Lansky

About This Book

If you're planning a U.S. or foreign trip, or if you just like to dream about going places, you'll find *Free Stuff for Travelers* an indispensable companion. Here's a book that lets you be your own travel agent. It's a catalog that describes over 1,000 maps, guidebooks, pamphlets, posters, catalogs and newsletters that you can get by mail from hundreds of tourist organizations, chambers of commerce, travel attractions, foreign tourist boards, motel chains and special vacation outfitters around the country. Whether you're interested in camping out in Wyoming, staying at a fancy hotel in New York, steamboating down the Mississippi or skiing in Switzerland, you'll find some source of information in this book that will help you plan your trip and make it more enjoyable.

And the best thing about planning your trip this way is that it won't cost you much. Most of the items listed in *Free Stuff for Travelers* are available for either a postcard or a self-addressed, stamped envelope. The rest will cost you no more than $1.00 for postage and handling and often less than 50¢.

To put this book together, we solicited materials from thousands of sources. We then evaluated everything we received, chose the best materials and secured a written pledge that the items listed here will be available through June 1982.

Though mistakes do happen, we've tried our best to make sure you get what you send for. And we would like to thank the organizations and associations listed here for their interest and help in making this book possible.

Note on government publications: We've been in close contact with the government agencies whose materials are listed in *Free Stuff for Travelers*, and we have every assurance that these publications will be available through June 1982. But because of

INTRODUCTION

the vagaries of government budgets and because of the volume of requests these agencies get, it's possible that some of their publications may be temporarily unavailable at certain times.

What's in This Book

In *Free Stuff for Travelers*, you'll find out how to send for

- maps, posters, calendars of events and guidebooks from hundreds of city and state tourist organizations around the country;
- pamphlets and foldouts about state and national parks, ski areas, zoos, amusement parks, museums, halls of fame, historical sites and festivals;
- travel information about cruises, sightseeing tours and special outdoors expeditions (for example, biking, backpacking and canoeing trips) in the U.S. and around the world;
- catalogs from mail-order camping equipment suppliers;
- guidebooks from foreign tourist boards;
- directories of hotels, motels, campgrounds and resorts;

- sample copies of travel magazines and newsletters; and
- booklets and pamphlets on such diverse subjects as dealing with emergencies on the road, packing, traveling with babies, travel for the handicapped, customs regulations and passports.

How to Use This Book

Please ask for only those materials that you really want or can use, and please follow these directions as precisely as you can. The organizations that supply the materials listed in this book are under no obligation to respond to requests that are improperly made.

- Please ask for only **one** copy of each item or packet of information you are interested in. Note to teachers: do not request classroom quantities of any of these materials.
- Make each request as brief as possible and always note what you've enclosed in the envelope you're sending.
- Ask for each publication by title or topic. In some cases you will be asked to request a "tourist information packet" about one location or

another. The contents of such a packet may vary, depending on the season or the availability of certain publications.

- In some cases, you'll be presented with a list of publications to choose from. You don't have to send a separate postcard or letter for each of them. Use one postcard or letter to list what you want—that way you'll save the organization you're contacting **and** yourself some time and postage.

- Always write your name and address on both the letter you send and the envelope you send it in. Gummed, self-addressed labels are ideal for this.

- If the directions ask you to send a postcard (and many do), please comply with them. Suppliers can answer your requests more promptly if you do, and it saves you postage money. (Remember that postcards must measure at least 3½" x 5½".)

- If the instructions say to send money, please enclose the fewest number of coins possible, and tape them to the letter you send so they won't rip or fall out of your envelope. (One piece of tape per coin is enough.) Please don't send stamps unless asked to.

- If you're asked to send a self-addressed, stamped envelope, it's very important that you fold up and enclose a business-size (at least 9"-long) envelope. In some cases you will be asked to stamp it with more than 1 stamp.

- Be prepared to wait 4 to 8 weeks for your materials to arrive. You could be surprised with a quicker reply, but you may also have to wait a little longer if a particular organization gets a lot of requests in a short period of time.

- Please do not ask Meadowbrook Press to send you any of the materials listed in *Free Stuff for Travelers.*

TRAVEL TIPS

TRAVEL TIPS

AAA

Three informative publications from the AAA (American Automobile Association).

- "American Automobile Association," a pamphlet, explains how AAA started and what services it offers today.
- "Your Driving Costs," a comprehensive pamphlet, helps you to figure out what it costs to own and operate a car. Includes space for your own computations.
- "Gas Watcher's Guide," a brief pamphlet, supplies specific advice on how to conserve gasoline.

Ask for: all 3 publications by name
Send: a 9" self-addressed envelope with 2 first-class stamps attached
To: American Automobile Assn.
Public Relations Dept.
8111 Gatehouse Rd.
Falls Church, VA 22042

Driving Aids

Two publications for drivers from the Federal Highway Administration: a map of the United States and Hawaii showing the system of interstate and defense highways and a color foldout with a key to international road signs, including those for services and recreation areas.

Ask for: "The National System of Interstate and Defense Highways" and "Road Symbol Signs"
Send: a postcard
To: Office of Public Affairs, HPA–1
Federal Highway Administration, DOT
400 Seventh St. SW
Washington, DC 20590

Saving Gas

An illustrated booklet about gasoline that explains how gasoline works in an automobile engine to produce power, how its components are blended and how to select the right grade of gasoline. Stresses the importance of keeping your car tuned and offers hints for getting good gasoline mileage. Also mentions where to get a booklet comparing the gas mileage for new cars.

Ask for: "Gasoline: More Miles Per Gallon"
Send: a postcard
To: Consumer Information Ctr.
Dept. 613J
Pueblo, CO 81009

DRIVING TIPS

- Avoid excessive high speed or jerky driving; learn to drive as smoothly and steadily as traffic and road conditions allow.
- Turn off your engine if you stop more than a minute. Restarting uses less gasoline than a minute's idling.
- Look ahead and pace yourself to minimize stops at traffic lights and jam-ups.

Save Gasoline

A fact sheet for automobile drivers about conserving gasoline. It suggests 8 ways to make sure you get every precious mile out of each gallon of gasoline, including driving techniques that save energy and car maintenance tips. Lists the approximate percentage of fuel that can be saved by using each suggestion.

Ask for: "Gasoline Fitness Plan"
Send: 25¢
To: Budget Rent a Car Corp.
Public Relations, Dept. H
35 E. Wacker Dr.
Chicago, IL 60601

SOME TIPS

- A running air conditioner can decrease gas mileage by 9 to 20 percent with stop-and-go driving in hot weather. Use it less.
- Driving with the windows closed reduces wind resistance and improves gas mileage. Use the vents for air circulation instead of opening windows.

Car Repair

A booklet about emergency car repairs. Explains how to diagnose and fix—at least temporarily—several problems that all too often leave unprepared motorists stranded. The booklet provides a list of basic items needed for emergency repairs and a clearly labeled diagram of an automobile engine, along with many other color illustrations.

Ask for: "The Emergency Repair Book" (#13)
Send: a postcard
To: Shell Oil Co.
P.O. Box 61609
Houston, TX 77208

Q & A

Q: Do I have to stop if the alternator light comes on?
A: No. This light means that the alternator is no longer recharging the battery, but you can still drive for a while on the battery's stored energy. If you have to go very far to reach a service station or garage, turn off electrical devices that can sap the battery's energy.

Car Breakdowns

A brief booklet to keep in your glove compartment that shows what to do if your car breaks down. It provides tips for when you get a flat tire, run out of gas or overheat your engine. In addition, it tells how to avoid a breakdown in the first place. Illustrated with color photographs, the booklet includes a checklist for prevention and many safety precautions.

Ask for: "The Breakdown Book" (#2)
Send: a postcard
To: Shell Oil Co.
P.O. Box 61609
Houston, TX 77208

Car Mechanics

A directory of car repair establishments that employ certified mechanics. Lists names, addresses and phone numbers of garages in which one or more mechanics has passed a written test given by the National Institute for Automotive Service Excellence. A directory is available for each state.

Ask for: "State Listing of Employers of NIASE Certified Members" (specify the state)
Send: a 9" self-addressed, stamped envelope
To: NIASE, Ste. 515
Free Stuff for Travelers
1825 K St. NW
Washington, DC 20006

Car Accidents

A booklet about car accidents—what to do if you see one, have one or cause one. The booklet explains where to stop your car, how to warn other cars, whether to move accident victims and more. Also covers some basic first-aid techniques and includes a list of items that make up an "accident kit."

Ask for: "The Accident Book" (#15)
Send: a postcard
To: Shell Oil Co.
P.O. Box 61609
Houston, TX 77208

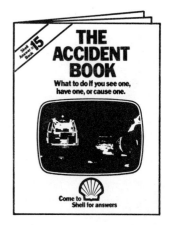

Emergencies

A valuable booklet for anyone who owns or drives a car. It explains how to deal with emergencies that can happen while you are driving, such as brake failure, fires, loss of lights, dropped driveshaft, flat tires, blowouts and more. Also offers suggestions to help you avoid such emergencies, along with checklists of first-aid and repair materials to carry in your car.

Ask for: "How to Deal with Motor Vehicle Emergencies"
Send: a postcard
To: Consumer Information Ctr.
Dept. 506J
Pueblo, CO 81009

HOOD POP-UP

Caution: A frequent cause of this problem is the failure of a service station attendant to close the hood properly after checking the oil, radiator or battery. You should get accustomed to the sound made by your hood when it is closed firmly. Thereafter, if you fail to hear the customary "thunk" when an attendant closes your hood, check the hood yourself before proceeding.

Emergencies

An informative booklet about driving emergencies. It tells what to do if your brakes don't work, a tire blows, your accelerator sticks, your car skids, your car falls into water, the hood flies up or a car is coming at you. The booklet is easy to read and is illustrated with color photographs. A preparedness checklist is included to help you avoid emergencies.

Ask for: "The Driving Emergency Book" (#7)
Send: a postcard
To: Shell Oil Co.
P.O. Box 61609
Houston, TX 77208

Foul Weather Driving

A booklet about driving in bad weather. It explains what to do if your car becomes snowbound, why a light rain can be even more dangerous than a downpour, why you should use low beams in fog and more. The booklet is illustrated with color photographs and includes a list for a basic winter emergency kit.

Ask for: "The Foul Weather Driving Book" (#11)
Send: a postcard
To: Shell Oil Co.
P.O. Box 61609
Houston, TX 77208

SAFETY TIPS

- In a light rain, use your windshield washers before you turn your wipers on. There may not be enough rainwater to wash the film off the windshield, resulting in streaking when you turn the wipers on. And that can greatly reduce your vision.
- If you must go through deep water, go slow. (Too fast and you may splash water on your ignition system, shorting out your spark plugs.)

TRAVEL TIPS

Alert Driving

A pamphlet for automobile drivers with valuable information about staying alert. Suggests 15 exercises that will relieve the tension and fatigue caused by driving in traffic or over long distances. Each exercise takes only 6 seconds, and most can be done while you're still sitting in your car. There are special exercises for neck, shoulders, back, thighs, hips and abdomen.

Ask for: "Staying Alert on the Highway"
Send: 25¢
To: Budget Rent a Car Corp.
Public Relations, Dept. H
35 E. Wacker Dr.
Chicago, IL 60601

Auto Tape Tour

A large foldout about a series of cassette tapes that provide guided tours to England, Ireland and national parks in the U.S. and Canada. The foldout describes the types of facts, history, legends and other tidbits each tape contains. Also includes maps, prices and ordering information.

Ask for: "CC Inc. Auto Tape Tours"
Send: 15¢
To: Comprehensive
Communications, Inc.
Dept. FST
P.O. Box 385
Scarsdale, NY 10583

Trailer Safety

An illustrated booklet for vacationers who own or rent camping or travel trailers. This booklet about trailer safety covers hitches, loading, brakes, safety chains and breakaway switches. Also contains a list of safety tips. A glossary is included.

Ask for: "Travel & Camper Trailer Safety"
Send: a postcard
To: Consumer Information Ctr.
Dept. 668H
Pueblo, CO 81009

Camping

A large foldout about public lands in the western states and Alaska where camping is allowed. The foldout lists over 200 locations—many of them accessible only through backpacking, horseback riding or boating—directions for getting there and information on what activities and facilities are available. Includes a map and notes on safety, water, hunting, fishing and more.

Ask for: "Camping on the Public Lands"
Send: a postcard
To: Consumer Information Ctr.
Dept. 613J
Pueblo, CO 81009

Winter Camping

A foldout for winter mountaineers and campers, designed to help beginners learn how to avoid the hazards of this rewarding sport. Provides tips on keeping warm and dry, finding and preparing campsites and choosing the correct clothing and equipment.

Ask for: "For the Winter Mountaineer"
Send: 15¢ and a 9" self-addressed, stamped envelope
To: Adirondack Mountain
Club, Inc.
172 Ridge St.
Glens Falls, NY 12801

TIPS
- Never travel alone. 4 is recommended minimum number; if injury occurs, one can attend victim while others go for help. Recommended maximum group size 8. Keep together and organized.
- Notify family or friend back home of plans, departure and return points, route and destination, and anticipated return time.

Hypothermia

A foldout with information on how hypothermia (a condition when your body loses more heat than it can produce) can kill a wet, fatigued, dehydrated person even during the summer. The foldout provides a chart of symptoms of each stage of hypothermia, along with suggested treatments.

Ask for: "For the Unprepared—Hypothermia, a Killer Companion"
Send: 15¢ and a 9" self-addressed, stamped envelope
To: Adirondack Mountain
Club, Inc.
172 Ridge St.
Glens Falls, NY 12801

TIPS
- Wear only **woolen** clothing. No jeans or corduroys.
- Wear layered clothing and adjust on or off as necessary.
- Take raingear.
- Keep back of neck warm.
- Carry spare set of socks and mittens.
- Eat regularly.
- Drink hot fluids.

TRAVEL TIPS

Frostbite

A foldout for winter sports lovers about frostbite. It describes the symptoms, prevention and treatment of the various stages of frostbite. Includes an explanation of what happens to body tissue when it freezes and the difference between "frostnip" (just the skin) and "frostbite" (the whole limb).

Ask for: "Frostbite"
Send: 15¢ and a 9" self-addressed, stamped envelope
To: Adirondack Mountain
    Club, Inc.
    172 Ridge St.
    Glens Falls, NY 12801

FROSTNIP

At the first signs of frostnip, rewarm the affected part at body temperature. Hands can be held in the crotch or armpit for warmth, or put them in the mouth. Feet can be rewarmed by placing them on the stomach of another group member. Holding a warm, dry hand over a cold ear or cheek will warm it rapidly. As warmth and color return, there is a tingling sensation.

Biting Bugs

A foldout for hikers and campers about the most common and bothersome insects one is likely to meet outdoors—the mosquito, ant, black fly, punkie, deer fly and bee. The foldout describes these insects and their bites, warns when and where they are prevalent and recommends methods to avoid painful bites.

Ask for: "Coping with Biting Trail Bugs of the Northeast"
Send: 15¢ and a 9" self-addressed, stamped envelope
To: Adirondack Mountain
    Club, Inc.
    172 Ridge St.
    Glens Falls, NY 12801

MOSQUITOES

This summer pest is not selective where it bites. If skin is exposed, that will suit the mosquito just fine. In fact, if it is hungry enough, it will gladly challenge your clothing by penetrating the weave with its elongated proboscis. Its bite is usually in the form of a moderately-sized white welt and itches for several hours. A good repellent often does the job, but be prepared with an ample supply.

Bears

A foldout for hikers and campers about black bears. It tells what to do and what not to do if you encounter a bear on the trail or near a campsite. It also explains how to store food so the smell won't attract bears and provides general background on black bears and their habits.

Ask for: "The Bear Facts"
Send: 15¢ and a 9" self-addressed, stamped envelope
To: Adirondack Mountain
    Club, Inc.
    172 Ridge St.
    Glens Falls, NY 12801

The Bear Facts

Wilderness

A foldout for wilderness hikers and campers. This general introduction contains tips about what to do before you go, while on the trip, while at the campsite, during cold weather and when trouble arises. It very briefly suggests safety precautions and necessary equipment.

Ask for: "Wilderness Tips"
Send: 15¢ and a 9" self-addressed, stamped envelope
To: Adirondack Mountain
Club, Inc.
172 Ridge St.
Glens Falls, NY 12801

HIKING TIPS

- Leave as much "hike out" time as you require to "hike in." Remember that darkness sets in early in the forest.
- Watch for trail markers. Carry and know how to use a good map and/or trailguide, and compass.
- Bushwhacking is a learned skill; make first trip with an experienced person. Never bushwhack alone.

Day Hiking

A foldout for the summertime day hiker. Provides tips on planning, packing and following trails, plus information on footgear, food, clothing, water, animals and plants. The foldout also lists safety precautions, including how to avoid hypothermia—a danger for overtired, wet and hungry hikers even in August.

Ask for: "For the Day Hiker"
Send: 15¢ and a 9" self-addressed, stamped envelope
To: Adirondack Mountain
Club, Inc.
172 Ridge St.
Glens Falls, NY 12801

CLOTHING

- Dress in layers so garments can be removed and donned to compensate for temperature, wind velocity, precipitation and sweating.
- Always take a windbreaker. Also take a woolen sweater, shirt or other garment with good insulating properties when wet. Wear during rest stops or on exposed summits to prevent chill. Sweatshirts are not recommended on the trail.

Backpacking

A foldout for the summer backpacker with helpful tips on planning and preparing for your trip; selecting equipment like packs, sleeping bags, tents and boots; choosing a campsite; finding and treating water; cooking and washing dishes. Also suggests what clothing and food to bring. Safety precautions are included.

Ask for: "For the Summer Backpacker"
Send: 15¢ and a 9" self-addressed, stamped envelope
To: Adirondack Mountain
Club, Inc.
172 Ridge St.
Glens Falls, NY 12801

THE PACK

Select a good quality, appropriately sized pack system, with waist or hip band, wide padded shoulder straps and small outside pockets for little items needed during hikes. Whether you use a pack frame or frameless system, be sure it is right for your height and body build. Avoid carrying more than 20% of your body weight.

TRAVEL TIPS

Hiking Trails

A packet of information from the International Backpackers' Association that includes an explanation of the association's objectives, a membership application, a brochure about survival in the wilderness, a catalog of publications about the wilderness and a foldout that explains the rules of trail etiquette.

Ask for: information packet
Send: $1.00
To: International Backpackers'
Assn. Inc.
P.O. Box 85
Lincoln Center, ME 04458

National Forests

A small foldout with a map showing the locations of all the National Forests and Grasslands in the country. Also gives the addresses of the regional offices of the Forest Service where you can write for further information on recreational opportunities at particular forests.

Ask for: "Field Offices of the Forest Service"
Send: a postcard
To: Forest Service
P.O. Box 2417
Washington, DC 20013

Canoes

A complete directory of the National Association of Canoe Liveries and Outfitters. It lists by state the addresses and phone numbers of places that rent canoes. Also lists manufacturers of canoes, kayaks, paddles and more. The directory explains the goals of the association and offers a subscription to *Canoe* magazine.

Ask for: "Official Rental Directory of Accredited Canoe Liveries and Outfitters"
Send: a postcard
To: NACLO
P.O. Box 515F
Big Rapids, MI 49307

TRAIL RULES

- Leave flowers, trees, rocks, snags, rivers, lakes and other natural features alone. Observe, enjoy and learn to appreciate all.
- Leave a camping area so that no one will ever know you were there.
- Have the courage and common sense to turn back in threatening weather. Don't risk your life foolishly.

Field Offices of the Forest Service
U.S. Department of Agriculture

NATIONAL ASSOCIATION
of
CANOE LIVERIES
and
OUTFITTERS

14

Water Sports

A packet of information from the U.S. Coast Guard covering a variety of subjects related to water sports, including boating, white water canoeing, houseboating and water skiing. The packet also contains safety information—pamphlets on distress signals, emergency repairs afloat, hypothermia and cold water survival.

Ask for: boating and safety pamphlets
Send: a postcard
To: Office of Boating, Public & Consumer Affairs, G–BA/TP–42 U.S. Coast Guard 2100 Second St. SW Washington, DC 20593

Government Publications

Seven catalogs of publications that are sold by the U.S. Government Printing Office. These catalogs list and describe the various booklets and pamphlets available on subjects relating to travel and recreation.

- "Recreational and Outdoor Activities" (SB017)
- "National Park Service Folder" (SB170)
- "Visitor Activities in the National Parks" (SB089)
- "Public Buildings, Landmarks and Historic Sites of the United States" (SB140)
- "Maps" (SB102)
- "Area Handbooks" (SB166) (on foreign countries)
- "Foreign Languages" (SB082)

Ask for: each catalog you want by name and number
Send: a postcard
To: Superintendent of Documents U.S. Government Printing Office Washington, DC 20402

HIGHLIGHTS

- "Camping: The National Forests, America's Playgrounds." A booklet about recreational opportunities available to campers in the National Forests.
- "National Parks of the Northeast." A colorful guide locating the parks with helpful information about each one.
- "National Park Service Guide to the Historic Places of the American Revolution." A guide to hundreds of revolutionary sites in 18 eastern states.
- "White House." A brief guide to the White House.
- "Angler's Guide to the U.S. Atlantic Coast." A publication with descriptions of each fishing area and its indigenous fish.

TRAVEL TIPS

Reminders

A foldout with 15 tips to follow when you're planning a trip. Covers such topics as canceling reservations, knowing your destination, packing and identifying your luggage, and keeping travel documents accessible. The foldout also explains the purpose and code of the American Society of Travel Agents.

Ask for: "15 Travel Reminders from ASTA"
Send: a 9" self-addressed, stamped envelope
To: ASTA Public Relations
711 Fifth Ave.
New York, NY 10022

Travel Agents

A foldout that explains what a travel agent is and suggests questions you should ask an agent when making arrangements. It also explains why you should choose an agent who is a member of the American Society of Travel Agents (ASTA), as well as the objectives of ASTA and the services it provides.

Ask for: "What Is a Travel Agent?"
Send: a 9" self-addressed, stamped envelope
To: ASTA Public Relations
711 Fifth Ave.
New York, NY 10022

Tour Operators

An extensive directory of tour operators from all over the world who belong to the United States Tour Operators Association—a group devoted to integrity in tourism. Gives the address and phone number of each operator, along with a list of the services available to consumers.

Ask for: "USTOA Membership Directory"
Send: a 9" self-addressed, stamped envelope
To: Mr. Robert E. Whitley
U.S. Tour Operators Assn.
2 W. 45th St., Ste. 1703
New York, NY 10036

SOME QUESTIONS

- What type of hotel accommodations are available? Are meals included? Is there a service charge?
- What do sightseeing tours include? Are they for a full day, or just part of the day? Are admission charges to museums included?
- What are the cancellation provisions?
- How soon should I make reservations to insure a space on a charter flight?

Packing

A packet of information that contains tips on selecting and packing a wardrobe to take on vacation. Also features advertisements for luggage with a price list and suggestions for choosing the right luggage for your needs. Several checklists—one for men, one for women and one with last-minute tips—are also included.

Ask for: "Tips on Packing Clothes for Travel"
Send: 50¢
To: Ventura T.C.
　　32-33 47th Ave.
　　Long Island City, NY 11101

Travel Clothes

An informative pamphlet about appropriate clothes for traveling. It offers hints on what clothes to take on a trip and how to pack them, along with advice on the proper clothing for various activities. Includes checklists for the kids, the whole family, men and women, although most of the pamphlet is directed toward women.

Ask for: "See America in Style—A Travel and Fashion Guide"
Send: a 9" self-addressed, stamped envelope
To: ILGWU
　　Union Label Dept.
　　22 W. 38th St.—MP
　　New York, NY 10018

A travel and fashion guide

Packing Tips

An informative excerpt on packing from *The Best European Travel Tips* by John Whitman. The excerpt gives suggestions on packing and traveling light to help you save time, money and trouble. Includes a traveler's checklist with down-to-earth advice on anything you might ever think of taking with you on a trip.

Ask for: "Packing Tips"
Send: 50¢
To: Packing Tips
　　P.O. Box 638FST
　　Wayzata, MN 55391

TRAVEL TIPS

Expert Hints

A foldout containing advice about traveling—particularly traveling abroad. Ten prominent travel writers and broadcasters from the U.S. and Canada give hints that have made their own trips easier and more enjoyable, covering everything from currency to cameras, from packing to passports.

Ask for: "More Travel Reminders from ASTA"
Send: a 9" self-addressed, stamped envelope
To: ASTA Public Relations
711 Fifth Ave.
New York, NY 10022

REST
Allow time when you arrive in order to rest and get accustomed to the new place. Don't try to rush out and see everything on the first day. Plan an hour or two of relaxation, preferably at the end of each afternoon, to pull yourself together. When you begin to droop, don't push yourself to see just one more museum, one more monument. Find the nearest cafe, restaurant or bar and decompress.

Lodging

A useful pamphlet about hotels, motels and resorts that explains what advantages and services each type of accommodation has to offer. Describes basic room types, price ranges, package plans, procedures for making reservations and more. Guidelines for tipping and hints for saving on food prices are also included.

Ask for: "Tips for Travelers"
Send: a 9" self-addressed, stamped envelope
To: American Hotel & Motel Assn.
888 Seventh Ave.
New York, NY 10019
Attn.: Public Relatons Dept.

Trips Abroad

A detailed pamphlet for those traveling abroad. This easy-to-read publication explains about passports, visas, tourist cards, insurance, customs, vaccinations, money, legal aid in foreign countries and much more. Includes additional sources of information and addresses of passport agencies. Blank pages for your own notes are provided in the back.

Ask for: "Your Trip Abroad"
Send: a postcard
To: Public Information Service
Room 4827A
U.S. Dept. of State
Washington, DC 20520

DRIVING
Some countries do not recognize a U.S. driver's license. Check with the embassy or consulate of the countries in which you plan to drive. Most countries do, however, accept an international driver's license. You can obtain one at a local office of an established automobile club. You will need 2 passport-size (2" X 2") photographs and your valid U.S. license. There is a fee.

TRAVEL TIPS

Going Overseas

A handy pamphlet for overseas travelers that contains general advice and several useful charts: time conversions for over 80 cities around the world, average temperatures during each month of the year for nearly 70 cities, tipping customs in 19 countries and clothing sizes for both men and women in America, Great Britain and Europe.

Ask for: "What Every Overseas Traveler Should Know"
Send: a 9" self-addressed, stamped envelope
To: ASTA Public Relations
711 Fifth Ave.
New York, NY 10022

> **JET LAG**
> You may suffer from "jet lag" when you cross 5 or more time zones. There are a number of things you can do to lessen the effects. Get as much sleep as you can on your flight. Eat and drink very lightly. Take it easy on the day you arrive. And as soon as possible, establish a routine in sync with local time.

Customs

A pamphlet about the customs procedures for U.S. citizens returning from abroad. It explains how to declare items, exemptions, penalties for undervaluing or failing to declare items, and prohibited or restricted items. A chart of duty rates for over 70 commonly purchased items is included, along with the addresses and phone numbers of customs offices.

Ask for: "Know Before You Go"
Send: a postcard
To: U.S. Customs Service
P.O. Box 7118
Washington, DC 20044

customs hints for returning u.s. residents

KNOW BEFORE YOU GO

Foreign Money

A pamphlet with tables of currency exchange rates for more than 60 countries, from Deak-Perera—the oldest, largest and most respected foreign currency exchange firm in the U.S. The tables give the names of money units for each country, along with the equivalents in U.S. dollars and cents.

Ask for: "Foreign Money Converter"
Send: a 9" self-addressed, stamped envelope
To: Deak-Perera
Attn.: B.H. Hessel
Marketing Dept.—FS
29 Broadway
New York, NY 10006

> **TIPPING**
> Hotels and restaurants in many countries add a service charge of 10 to 15 percent to your bill. You should ask if service is included when you are given the bill. If it isn't, a good rule of thumb is 15 percent for waiters. For chambermaids, concierges and other hotel employees, ask what is normally expected for tipping at the desk of the hotel. Or check with your airline or guide book.

Air Travel

An informative pamphlet about flying, especially for the first-time traveler. It explains how to make reservations, how to buy a ticket, how to fly abroad, how to fly with children or pets, what to do with your baggage, and more. Also covers flying for the handicapped.

Ask for: "How to Fly"
Send: a 9" self-addressed, stamped envelope
To: Public Relations
Air Transport Assn.
1709 New York Ave. NW
Washington, DC 20006

TICKETS

When you make a reservation by phone, you will be asked when you would like to pick up your ticket. It may be picked up either at an airline ticket office or at the airport when you check in for your flight. Should you make a reservation through a travel agent, set the date for ticket pick-up with the agent.

Air Rights

A comprehensive pamphlet for airline passengers, with information about their rights and about airline practices and regulations. It covers air fares, overbooking, delayed and canceled flights, baggage, smoking and safety. Also explains how and to whom to complain if something goes wrong. Provides addresses for the field offices of the Civil Aeronautics Board.

Ask for: "Fly-Rights"
Send: a postcard
To: Consumer Information Ctr.
Dept. 615J
Pueblo, CO 81009

SAFETY

Make sure all of your carry-on luggage will fit under the seat in front of you. Not all planes have storage areas in the passenger cabin, and if you try to carry too much with you, the crew may insist that you check in some items—and for good reason. A bag that is not properly stowed could turn into an unguided missile in an accident or block the aisles during an evacuation.

Flying Trouble

A helpful pamphlet for airline passengers. It gives advice on what to do when your luggage is lost, damaged or stolen, when you are bumped from a flight or when you have other problems with airlines. Published by a consumer protection agency, it contains facts about airline practices and regulations, discount fares and more.

Ask for: "Facts & Advice for Airline Passengers"
Send: a 9" self-addressed, stamped envelope
To: ACAP
P.O. Box 19029
Washington, DC 20036

Facts & Advice For Airline Passengers

"WE PUT THE BITE INTO PASSENGER RIGHTS"

Seniors

A foldout containing travel tips for senior citizens who plan to travel abroad. Provides helpful information on passports, clothing, money, health precautions and more. Addresses to write to for publications with more detailed information are also included.

Ask for: "Travel Tips for Senior Citizens"
Send: a postcard
To: Public Information Service
Room 4827A
U.S. Dept. of State
Washington, DC 20520

Park Passes

A foldout for people planning to visit federal parks and recreation areas. It explains how and where to get Golden Eagle and Golden Age Passports (entrance permits). The Golden Age Passport (for people over 62) is free. The foldout describes entrance, recreation and usage fees.

Ask for: "Golden Eagle, Golden Age Passports"
Send: a postcard
To: Consumer Information Ctr.
Dept. 616J
Pueblo, CO 81009

Accessibility

An informative booklet for the handicapped traveler that lists design features, facilities and services for the handicapped at 282 airport terminals in 40 countries. The booklet also provides travel tips and addresses that can supply more information about travel and accessibility for the handicapped.

Ask for: "Access Travel: Airports"
Send: a postcard
To: Consumer Information Ctr.
Dept. 612J
Pueblo, CO 81009

Travel Tips for Senior Citizens

GOLDEN EAGLE

The Golden Eagle Passport is an annual entrance permit to parks, monuments and recreation areas administered by the Federal Government. It admits the permit holder and carload of accompanying people. Where entry is not by private car, the Golden Eagle Passport admits the permit holder and family group— parents, children and spouse.

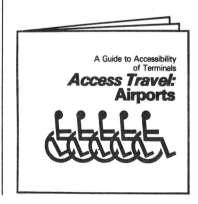

A Guide to Accessibility of Terminals
Access Travel: Airports

TRAVEL TIPS

Student Travel

A catalog for traveling students from the Council on International Educational Exchange. It's packed with information about student travel bargains around the world—student flights, rail and car transportation, work-abroad programs, budget accommodations and unique tours. Also contains an application form for an International Student I.D. card.

Ask for: "Student Travel Catalog"
Send: 50¢
To: CIEE
Dept. STCMBP
205 E. 42nd St.
New York, NY 10017

Babies

A helpful booklet for people with babies who want to take them along on their travels. Reprinted from the book, *No-Nonsense Nutrition for Your Baby's First Year,* it tells what foods to take shopping, camping, on car trips and to other places. Also suggests foods that you can order in restaurants for your baby to eat.

Ask for: "Traveling with Your Baby"
Send: $1.00
To: CBI Publishing Co.
Attn.: Chris B. Ives, Dept. FST
51 Sleeper St.
Boston, MA 02210

AIRLINE TRAVEL

- Most airlines require a baby to be 6 weeks old before flying.
- Airlines (Amtrak too!) allow children under 2 to travel free of charge.
- Most large airports have special nursing or baby areas in the ladies' lounge; Kennedy boasts of a rocking chair in theirs.

Travel Games

An entertaining booklet of travel games for families traveling by car. Packed full of games for children and adults, it is designed to make the trip more relaxed and enjoyable. Most of the games are of the treasure hunt type; the players look for objects or words on signs along the road.

Ask for: "Travel Games"
Send: $1.00 (15¢ will be refunded)
To: The Beavers
Star Rte., P.O. Box 184
Laporte, MN 56461

Travel/Holiday

A current issue of *Travel/Holiday* magazine. This magazine has insider's tips on special events, important changes and developments in travel, monthly recipes, stories on places from Baltimore to Luxembourg, color photographs of people and places and much more. Includes information on many tours. You'll receive a 50¢ credit if you decide to subscribe to the magazine.

Ask for: current issue of *Travel/Holiday*
Send: 50¢
To: Travel/Holiday
    Travel Bldg., Rm. 3A
    Floral Park, NY 11001

International Travel News

A sample copy of the monthly publication, *International Travel News.* Written for those who travel frequently, this newsletter offers up-to-date reports from readers. Articles cover both bargain and deluxe travel. There are special sections about airlines, charters, cruises, tours, hotels, shopping, health, culture and more.

Ask for: *International Travel News*
Send: a postcard
To: Armond M. Noble
    Intl. Travel News
    2120 28th St.
    Sacramento, CA 95818

Travelore Report

A sample issue of the newsletter, *The Travelore Report.* Offers short articles about vacation destinations (many of them for bargain rates) and about inexpensive ways to travel. A section of travel tips brings readers up to date on air fares to Italy, lodgings in Vail, food fairs in Paris and more.

Ask for: *The Travelore Report*
Send: 90¢
To: Travelore Report
    Dept. FST
    225 S. 15th St.
    Philadelphia, PA 19102

TRAVEL TIPS

Joyer Travel Report

A newsletter that stresses bargains in travel, both in the U.S. and around the world. *Joyer Travel Report* relates news about travel costs, tips on economical charters and reviews of hotels and restaurants. The "Travelers' Exchange" allows subscribers to swap ideas, homes, services and more.

Ask for: current issue of *Joyer Travel Report*
Send: $1.00
To: Ms. Lynn Smithe
Joyer Travel Report
7315 Wisconsin Ave.,
Ste. 1200N
Bethesda, MD 20014

The Jogger

A directory of hotels across the country that offer jogging facilities on site or provide maps to safe trails nearby. Originally published in the National Jogging Association's newsletter, *The Jogger,* it is organized alphabetically by state. In addition to providing addresses, phone numbers and rates for the hotels, the directory briefly describes the jogging facilities.

Ask for: "NJA's Hotel Survey"
Send: 50¢
To: Hotel Survey
NJA
2420 K St. NW
Washington, DC 20037

SAFETY

Safety is an important consideration for every traveler, especially when running in strange territory. Whenever possible, run with a partner, and schedule your workouts for daylight hours. When running in cities, stick to the maps and marked trails until you know your way around, and obey the local pedestrian traffic laws.

Travel Smart

A sample copy of a newsletter about bargain travel, especially in the Caribbean. Many articles in *Travel Smart* reveal the cheapest fares to islands in the Caribbean, to U.S. cities and elsewhere. Some articles suggest restaurants and alternative hotels. The newsletter also offers special discounts to subscribers on cruises, lodging, rental cars and more.

Ask for: *Travel Smart*
Send: $1.00
To: H.J. Teison
Travel Smart
40 Beechdale Rd.
Dobbs Ferry, NY 10522

UNITED STATES

ALABAMA

Alabama

An assortment of items and publications about Alabama, including a small plastic pin in the shape of the state, a red felt Alabama sticker and the publications listed below. In addition, the Bureau will be glad to provide information on any area of the state or any special interests that you specify.

- "Alabama the Beautiful," a large booklet that discusses the attractions, museums, historical sites, recreational activities and special events in each of the 3 regions of the state. Also lists the public and private campgrounds and their facilities.
- "Official Alabama Highway Map" marks tourist attractions in the state and includes street maps of the major cities.
- "Alabama Calendar of Events," a large pamphlet published quarterly, describes exhibits, concerts, festivals and other special events occurring all over the state. Also lists attractions and museums.

Ask for: pin, sticker and/or each publication you want by name
Send: a postcard

To: Alabama Bureau of Publicity & Information
532 S. Perry St.
Montgomery, AL 36130

CITIES

Birmingham

- "Dandy Places to Visit in the Greater Birmingham Area," a large pamphlet that describes museums, historical sites, parks and attractions, with a map to locate them. Also mentions festivals and special events.
- "Daytime Nighttime Good-time Guide to Birmingham," a foldout that includes a map, pictures and descriptions of the city's highlights.
- "Calendar," published monthly with details of each day's events. (Specify the month you are interested in.)
- "Greater Birmingham Hotel/Motel Guide," a foldout that provides a list of local accommodations.
- "Restaurant Guide," a foldout that supplies a list of local eating establishments.

Ask for: each publication you want by name

Send: a postcard
To: Greater Birmingham Convention & Visitors' Bureau
Commerce Ctr., 2027 First Ave. N
Birmingham, AL 35203

Talladega

- "Visit Talladega," a pamphlet that lists major sights and events.
- "Talladega City Map."
- "Winston 500 Grand National Stock Car Race," a pamphlet about a major car race.
- "Talladega 500 Grand National Stock Car Race," a pamphlet with information about another local car race.

Ask for: all 4 publications by name
Send: a 9" self-addressed envelope with 2 first-class stamps attached
To: Chamber of Commerce Travel Dept.
P.O. Drawer A
Talladega, AL 35160

PARKS & PUBLIC LANDS

State Parks

Two publications about the Alabama State Parks. A direc-

tory to the 21 parks describes their campgrounds, resort areas, recreational facilities and activities. The other pamphlet lists the rates for cabins, resort rooms and campgrounds and tells about recreational activities in the parks.
Ask for: "Alabama State Parks" and "Alabama State Parks Accommodation and Activities Information"
Send: a postcard
To: Alabama State Parks
64 N. Union St., Box FS
Montgomery, AL 36130

RESORTS

Grand Hotel
A packet of information about the Grand Hotel, located on Mobile Bay. A color fold-out emphasizes golf, tennis and other available sports; a map outlines the grounds; and a reprint from *Golf* magazine describes the resort's attractions and historical backgrounds.
Ask for: information on the Grand Hotel
Send: a postcard
To: Thomas Keith Richardson
Grand Hotel
P.O. Box TKR
Pt. Clear, AL 36564

HISTORICAL SITES

Bellingrath Gardens
A colorful foldout about the Bellingrath gardens and home, a few miles south of Mobile. The foldout describes the rooms, art, china, furnishings and formal and Oriental gardens on the estate. A map and directions are provided.
Ask for: "Bellingrath Gardens and Home"
Send: a postcard
To: Bellingrath Gardens
Rte. 1, Box 60
Theodore, AL 36582

Chattahoochee Trace
A booklet that outlines 6 mini-tours along the Chattahoochee Trace, which follows the river of the same name through Alabama and Georgia. Each tour takes several days and requires no more than 1 tank of gasoline. And each includes parks, museums and other attractions, as well as many places of historical interest.
Ask for: "Chattahoochee Trace Mini-Tour Guide"
Send: a postcard

To: Chattahoochee
Dept. MP
P.O. Box 33
Eufaula, AL 36027

Alaska
A full-color booklet that includes descriptions of Alaska's federal and state parklands, key cities and major geographical areas. Also contains a comprehensive travel directory of services, attractions, tours, accommodations and outdoor activities in Alaska and Canada's Yukon region.
Ask for: "Worlds of Alaska and Canada's Yukon"
Send: a postcard
To: Worlds of Alaska
Alaska Div. of Tourism
Pouch E
Juneau, AK 99811

PARKS & PUBLIC LANDS

Bureau of Land Management
A number of foldouts describing recreational opportunities available on Alaskan land managed by the U.S. Bureau of Land Management. Some of these pub-

lications list campsites and trails, while others describe facilities along highways through public lands.

Ask for: information you want on specific topics or regions
Send: a postcard
To: U.S. Dept. of the Interior
Bureau of
Land Management
Alaska State Office
701 C St.
P.O. Box 13
Anchorage, AK 99513

Arizona

A colorful booklet about the state of Arizona. Outlines hundreds of things to do and places to visit, including campgrounds, parks, attrac-

tions, historical sites and ski areas.

Ask for: "Arizona"
Send: a postcard
To: Arizona Office of Tourism
Dept. FS
112 N. Central Ave.
Phoenix, AZ 85004

REGIONS

Valley of the Sun

A full-color guide to the Valley of the Sun, a region in and around Phoenix that includes Scottsdale and Tempe. Much information is included about hotels, motels, restaurants, airlines, museums and attractions in this region.

Ask for: "Valley Visitors' Guide"
Send: $1.00
To: Phoenix & Valley of the Sun
Convention & Visitors'
Bureau
Visitors' Information,
Dept. D–100
2701 E. Camelback
Phoenix, AZ 85016

CITIES

Lake Havasu City

A colorful foldout about this resort city that features his-

toric London Bridge. Lake Havasu City is near the Arizona-California border, about halfway between Phoenix and Las Vegas.

Ask for: "Royal Resort"
Send: a 9" self-addressed, stamped envelope
To: "Sunny"
Lake Havasu Area
Chamber of Commerce
2074 McCulloch Blvd.
Lake Havasu City,
AZ 86403

PARKS & PUBLIC LANDS

Bureau of Land Management

A variety of publications about recreational opportunities available on land managed by the Arizona state office of the U.S. Bureau of Land Management. Some list facilities and activities at campgrounds and recreational areas; others provide information on hiking in primitive areas. A catalog of outdoor recreation maps is also available.

Ask for: information you want on specific topics or regions
Send: a postcard

To: U.S. Dept. of the Interior
Bureau of Land
Management
Arizona State Office
2400 Valley Bank Ctr.
Phoenix, AZ 85073

SKI AREAS

Flagstaff

Three publications about ski resorts near Flagstaff, including one open in the summer as well as the winter.

- "Arizona Snow Bowl Ski"
- "Arizona Snow Bowl Summer"
- "Mt. Holly Ski Resort"

Ask for: all 3 publications by name
Send: a 9" self-addressed envelope with 2 first-class stamps attached
To: Northland Recreation, Inc.
P.O. Box 158
Flagstaff, AZ 86002

Arkansas

A packet of information about the state of Arkansas that includes a highway map; a directory of state parks; a brochure about autumn activities; special coupons for reduced rates at motels, museums and more; and a tour guide that lists motels, re-

sorts, museums and other attractions.

Ask for: "The Vacation Kit"
Send: a postcard
To: Arkansas Dept. of Parks
& Tourism
1 Capitol Mall
Little Rock, AR 72201

CAMPGROUNDS

A packet of information that contains a guide to the facilities at over 260 government-operated campgrounds plus some private sites. Includes general information on travel in the state.

Ask for: "The Camper's Kit"
Send: a postcard
To: Arkansas Dept. of Parks
& Tourism
1 Capitol Mall
Little Rock, AR 72201

ATTRACTIONS

Blanchard Springs Cavern/Ozark Folk Center

A foldout about the Blanchard Springs Cavern and the Ozark Folk Center, both located in Stone County in north-central Arkansas. The

foldout describes the tours through the caverns (one available to handicapped persons) and the crafts and mountain music that visitors can see performed at the center. A calendar of events is also available.

Ask for: "The Natural Attractions in Arkansas" and "The Calendar of Operations"
Send: a postcard
To: Ozark Mountain Ctr.—MP
Mountain View, AR 72560

California

REGIONS

Lake Tahoe

- "Tahoe Travelers' Almanac," a directory that lists motels, hotels, condominiums, ski resorts, recreation areas, campgrounds and entertainment spots.
- "Discover Facts about South Lake Tahoe," a fact sheet that offers general information.

Ask for: each publication you want by name
Send: a postcard
To: South Lake Tahoe Visitors'
Bureau
P.O. Box 17727
South Lake Tahoe, CA 95706
Attn.: Travelers' Information

CALIFORNIA

Long Beach

A packet of information and maps about the greater Long Beach and Orange County area just south of Los Angeles. Describes where to stay and what to see, as well as some emergency services.

Ask for: tourist information packet about Greater Long Beach and Orange County
Send: $1.00
To: Travelers Aid Soc.—FST
449 E. Broadway
Long Beach, CA 90802

Redwood Empire

A booklet guiding tourists through the Redwood Empire, which stretches 400 miles from San Francisco into Oregon. It provides detailed maps and information on hotels and motels, parks, campgrounds, museums and wineries. Special attention is given to the sights in San Francisco.

Ask for: "Redwood Empire Visitors Guide"
Send: $1.00
To: Redwood Empire Assn.
360 Post St., Ste. 401
San Francisco, CA 94108

Santa Clarita

A booklet about the Santa Clarita Valley, near Los Angeles. It offers historical information about the area, a small map and a directory to 45 attractions, historical sites and other points of interest.

Ask for: "Santa Clarita Valley Community Guide"
Send: $1.00
To: Santa Clarita Valley
Chamber of Commerce
24275 Walnut Ave.
Newhall, CA 91321

Shasta Lake

- "Shasta Lake Map" (25¢), a detailed area map that includes hiking trails, campgrounds and travel tips.
- "Vacation Shasta Lake" (25¢), a foldout listing the facilities at area resorts, motels and campgrounds.
- "Fishing Tips for Shasta Lake" (25¢), a foldout with fishing advice.

Ask for: each publication you want by name
Send: the amount specified for each publication
To: Shasta Dam Area
Chamber of Commerce—MP
P.O. Box 1368
Central Valley, CA 96019

COUNTIES

Lake

Three publications about Lake County, located about 100 miles north of San Francisco.

- "Lake County Directory," a tabloid that describes the facilities at resorts and campgrounds and includes some historical and legendary background of the area.
- "Things to Do in Lake County," a map that provides directions to antique shops, boat rentals, dancing, parks and festivals.
- "Clear Lake," a reprint of an article from *Motorland* magazine, which reviews the area's resorts and attractions.

Ask for: each publication you want by name
Send: a postcard
To: Lake County Chamber of Commerce
875 M Lakeport Blvd.
Lakeport, CA 95453

Madera

A foldout with maps and color photographs of Madera County, located in the heart of California. It invites visitors to 6 annual festivals.

Ask for: "Madera County—The Pleasure Is Yours"
Send: a 9" self-addressed, stamped envelope
To: Madera Chamber of Commerce
P.O. Box 307
Madera, CA 93639

Sonoma

Two colorful foldouts about this county and its major city, Santa Rosa. These publications direct visitors to local attractions, wineries, recreation areas, parks, restaurants and accommodations.

Ask for: "Santa Rosa, Sonoma County" and "California's Metro Santa Rosa Travelers' Guide"
Send: a postcard
To: Chamber of Commerce
637 First St.
Santa Rosa, CA 95404

CITIES

Beverly Hills

- "Where It's at Guide," a pamphlet that explains where to shop, dine and stay.
- "A Day in Beverly Hills," a pamphlet that invites visitors to take personalized tours.
- "Rodeo Drive Map."
- "Beverly Hills Map."
- "Beverly Hills," a foldout that describes the city's climate and major attractions.

Ask for: each publication you want by name
Send: a postcard

To: Beverly Hills Visitors' Bureau
239 S. Beverly Dr.
Beverly Hills, CA 90212

Leggett

A foldout about this Redwood County town plus a postcard of the famous local redwood tree that has an automobile tunnel running through it.

Ask for: "Where's Leggett?" and "Tree Postcard"
Send: a 9" self-addressed, stamped envelope
To: Leggett Valley Chamber of Commerce
P.O. Box 56
Leggett, CA 95455

Los Angeles

- "Los Angeles Guide" ($1.00), a large and comprehensive booklet that briefs visitors on festivals, events, attractions, shopping , hotels, airlines and much more.
- "Only in L.A." (free), a pamphlet that briefly lists some of the above information.
- "Getting Around in Los Angeles and Southern California" (free), a map of Los Angeles and Orange Counties.
- "Date Lines" (free), a calendar published every 2 months.
- "Greater Los Angeles Ac-

commodations" (free), a guide to hotels and motels.
- "Greater Los Angeles Dining" (free), a pamphlet that lists restaurants and the address, price range and specialties of each.

Ask for: each publication you want by name
Send: a postcard for the free publications; the amount specified for any others
To: Greater Los Angeles Visitors' & Convention Bureau
Visitor Inquiry
505 Flower St.
Los Angeles, CA 90071

Los Gatos

- "Good Times in Los Gatos" (50¢ and a 9" self-addressed, stamped envelope), a foldout with color photos and tidbits on the historical sites, shopping spots and parks of the area.
- "Lodging Guide" and "Restaurant Guide" (a 9" self-addressed, stamped envelope), 2 small foldouts that list local hotels and eating spots.

Ask for: each publication you want by name
Send: whatever is specified for each
To: Los Gatos Chamber of Commerce
P.O. Box 1820
Los Gatos, CA 95031

CALIFORNIA

Modesto

Three publications on this city halfway between San Francisco and Yosemite.

- "Modesto—On the Way Wherever You Go," a foldout that offers maps of the city and the area and describes festivals, parks and more.
- "Modesto—On the Way to Yosemite," a foldout that outlines 4 routes to Yosemite.
- "Modesto Mini Tours," a foldout that lists tours about parks, wildflowers, gourmet food, lakes and the gold country.

Ask for: each publication you want by name
Send: a postcard
To: Modesto Chamber of
  Commerce—FS
  P.O. Box 844
  Modesto, CA 95353

Palm Springs

A packet of information about this Southern California city. A hotel directory tells you what to wear and where to play tennis and golf; it also describes the facilities, policies and rates of hotels and motels in the area. Also included are an information card about the Aerial Tramway and a card for requesting information on special, small hotels.

Ask for: "Sunny Packet"
Send: a postcard
To: Palm Springs Convention
  & Visitors' Bureau
  Dept. MB—8
  Municipal Airport
  Palm Springs, CA 92262

San Diego

A foldout with color photographs and descriptions of San Diego's sights: the zoo, Sea World, museums, beaches, historical sites and more.

Ask for: "San Diego"
Send: a postcard
To: San Diego Convention &
  Visitors' Bureau
  Dept. FST
  1200 Third Ave., Ste. 824
  San Diego, CA 92101

San Francisco

Two publications to help visitors plan their vacations to the Golden Gate City: a lodging guide that lists hotels and motels according to the area of the city and a calendar published 3 times a year describing music, theater, art, sports, special events and sightseeing tours.

Ask for: "San Francisco Lodging Guide" and "San Francisco Coming Events & Sightseeing"
Send: a postcard

To: San Francisco Visitor
  Information Ctr.
  Dept. FS
  Halladie Plaza
  900 Market St.
  San Francisco, CA 94102

PARKS & PUBLIC LANDS

Bureau of Land Management

Information about recreational opportunities on public lands in California. Lists campgrounds managed by the U.S. Bureau of Land Management and the hiking

32

and white-water canoeing available in the various recreation areas.

Ask for: information about recreational use of public lands
Send: a postcard
To: U.S. Dept. of the Interior
Bureau of Land Management
California State Office
Federal Office Bldg.,
Rm. E–2841
2800 Cottage Way
Sacramento, CA 95825

State Parks

A directory to the state park system in California. It provides a California map, as well as detailed directions to each park and a chart describing various activities and facilities.

Ask for: "Guide to the California State Park System"
Send: $1.00
To: Distribution Ctr.
Dept. of Parks & Recreation
P.O. Box 2390
Sacramento, CA 95811

Yosemite National Park

A packet of information on accommodations and outdoor recreational opportunities throughout the year at this national park.

Ask for: information on Yosemite National Park
Send: a postcard

To: Marketing Dept.—FS
Yosemite Park & Curry Co.
Yosemite National Park,
CA 95389

SKI AREAS

Ski Tahoe

A sample copy of the Nordic Ski Center's newsletter with a map of cross-country ski trails at Lake Tahoe.

Ask for: "Nordic Newsletter and Trail Map"
Send: a 9" self-addressed, stamped envelope
To: Tahoe Nordic Ski Ctr.
P.O. Box 1632
Tahoe City, CA 95730

ATTRACTIONS

Cannery

A foldout about this historic building, located in San Francisco's Fisherman's Wharf area. It has been converted into shops, restaurants, a theater and art galleries. The foldout offers maps of the area and directions for getting there by car or public transportation.

Ask for: "The Cannery"
Send: a postcard

To: The Cannery
2801 Leavenworth St.
San Francisco, CA 94133

Magic Mountain

A colorful foldout describing the rides and shows at Six Flags Magic Mountain, an amusement park just 25 minutes north of Hollywood.

Ask for: "Six Flags Magic Mountain"
Send: a postcard
To: Travel/Tour Sales Dept.
Six Flags Magic Mountain
P.O. Box 5500
Valencia, CA 91355

Marriott's Great America

A foldout about this attraction in Santa Clara, 45 minutes south of San Francisco. Describes the many types of crafts, food, theatrical performances and rides you'll find there.

Ask for: "Marriott's Great America"
Send: a 9" self-addressed, stamped envelope
To: Marriott's Great America
Sales Office—Free Stuff
P.O. Box 1776
Santa Clara, CA 95052

San Diego Zoo

Two foldouts about the San Diego Zoo and Wild Animal Park, including information on hours and admission prices.

COLORADO

Ask for: "San Diego Zoo" and "San Diego Wild Animal Park"
Send: a 9" self-addressed, stamped envelope
To: San Diego Zoo
Public Relations Dept.
Zoo & Wild Animal Park Brochure
P.O. Box 551
San Diego, CA 92112

Sea World

A colorful foldout on San Diego's Sea World. Features a map and general information on admission prices and hours.
Ask for: "Sea World"
Send: a 9" self-addressed, stamped envelope
To: Sea World Brochure
Marketing Dept.
Sea World
1720 S. Shores Rd.
San Diego, CA 92109

Universal Studios

A brief foldout describing the Universal Studios Tour, located in Los Angeles. Includes price and admission information with directions for finding the studios.
Ask for: "Take the Universal Studios Tour"
Send: a postcard
To: Tour Publicity Office
Universal Studios Tour
100 Universal City Plaza
Universal City, CA 91608

MUSEUMS

Exploratorium

A foldout about the Exploratorium in San Francisco's Marina district near the Golden Gate Bridge. Explains the museum's underlying theme of human perception and discusses its exhibits in the fields of science and technology.
Ask for: "Exploratorium—Everyone's Do-It-Yourself Museum"
Send: a 9" self-addressed, stamped envelope
To: Public Information Office
Exploratorium
3601 Lyon St.
San Francisco, CA 94123

Museum of Science & Industry

An exhibit directory for the museum of Science and Industry, off the Harbor Freeway in Los Angeles. The directory provides lists of exhibits and maps.
Ask for: "Exhibit Directory"
Send: a postcard
To: Museum of Science & Industry
Public Relations Dept.
700 State Dr.,
Exposition Park
Los Angeles, CA 90037

Colorado

COUNTIES

Pikes Peak

Two publications outlining things to do and see in Pikes Peak County, west of Colorado Springs. A visitors' guide describes museums, attractions, festivals, special events, motels and hotels, restaurants and more. A sample issue of *Pikes Peak County Magazine* reviews many of the attractions in the area.
Ask for: "A Visitors' Guide to Pikes Peak County, Colorado" and/or *Pikes Peak County Magazine*
Send: a 9" self-addressed, stamped envelope (Visitors' Guide); 75¢ (magazine)
To: Pikes Peak—Dept. 1
Ste. 430
Holly Sugar Bldg.
Colorado Springs, CO 80903

PARKS & PUBLIC LANDS

Bureau of Land Management

A variety of publications about recreational oppor-

tunities available on land managed by the Colorado state office of the U.S. Bureau of Land Management. Some publications list campsites and trails.
Ask for: information you want on specific topics or regions
Send: a postcard
To: U.S. Dept. of the Interior
Bureau of Land Management
Rm. 700, Colorado State
Bank Bldg.
1600 Broadway
Denver, CO 80202

State Parks

A foldout guide to Colorado's state parks and recreation areas. Provides a map, descriptions of the areas and a chart of the facilities and activities available in nearly 30 parks.
Ask for: "Guide to Colorado's State Parks & Recreation Areas"
Send: a postcard
To: Colorado Div. of Parks
& Outdoor Recreation
1313 Sherman St., #618
Denver, CO 80203

RESORTS

Steamboat Springs

Two colorful foldouts on winter and summer activities at this recreation area in north-western Colorado. The first foldout highlights the area's skiing facilities and includes a list of available accommodations. The reverse side folds out to a 18" x 24" poster of a winter mountain scene. Another foldout describes the summer activities at the Steamboat Village resort, including golf, tennis and family vacations. Also lists hotel and condominium rates and travel information.
Ask for: "Steamboat" and "The Steamboat Summer"
Send: a postcard
To: Steamboat Ski Corp.
Marketing Dept.
P.O. Box 1178
Steamboat Springs,
CO 80477

SKI AREAS

A directory listing every ski area in Colorado. Includes information on the exact location of the resort, its operating hours, the various elevations of available slopes, the lift races, ski schools, rental schedules and accommodations.
Ask for: "Colorado Ski Country USA"
Send: $1.00

To: Guide to Colorado Ski
Country USA
1410 Grant St.
Denver, CO 80203

Connecticut

- "Your Connecticut Vacation Guide," a large booklet full of color photographs and information on museums, historical sites, attractions, events, campgrounds, golf courses and other recreational opportunities in this seaboard state.
- "Connecticut Official Map," a map of the state (with inserts of the major cities) plus a description of selected attractions and a

list of boat-launching sites, ski areas and state parks.

Ask for: each publication you want by name
Send: a postcard
To: Connecticut Dept. of Economic Development—MP
210 Washington St.
Hartford, CT 06106

REGIONS

Northeast

A packet of information about the northeastern part of Connecticut, including a directory of private campgrounds all over the state, a map of the northeastern area and more general information.

Ask for: tourist information packet about northeast Connecticut
Send: a postcard
To: Connecticut Dept. of Economic Development—MP
210 Washington St.
Hartford, CT 06106

CITIES

Hartford

Three publications about the capital of Connecticut.

- "Greater Hartford Visitors' Guide," an extensive pamphlet that features attractions in Hartford and the surrounding area. Also describes local restaurants and lists accommodations and services in the area.
- "Greater Hartford City Streets and Highways," a map of the greater Hartford area plus a detailed map of the downtown.
- "The Walk—Hartford," a foldout that gives a self-guided tour through downtown Hartford. Includes a map and information about sites along the way.

Ask for: each publication you want by name
Send: a postcard
To: Greater Hartford Convention & Visitors' Bureau
1 Civic Center Plaza
Hartford, CT 06103

New Haven

A large packet of information about New Haven. Includes information on cruises, the area's history, museums, restaurants, hotels and motels and numerous attractions.

Ask for: tourist information packet about New Haven
Send: $1.00
To: Greater New Haven Chamber of Commerce
Dept. of Tourism Information
P.O. Box 1445
New Haven, CT 06506

PARKS & PUBLIC LANDS

State Parks

A pamphlet that describes in detail the recreational opportunities at the various state parks and forests in Connecticut. Also a foldout that lists available camping facilities and gives general information on camping in state parks.

Ask for: "Recreation in State Parks and Forests" and "Camping Connecticut"
Send: a postcard
To: Office of Parks & Recreation
165 Capitol Ave.
Hartford, CT 06115

Delaware

PARKS & PUBLIC LANDS

State Parks

A comprehensive foldout about Delaware's state parks and fish and wildlife areas, "Delaware Outdoors" provides descriptions, a state map and a chart of the facilities. Foldouts about the following individual parks are also available.

- Lum's Pond
- Cape Henlopen
- Delaware Seashore
- Killens Pond
- Fort Delaware

Ask for: "Delaware Outdoors" and information on specific parks you are interested in
Send: a postcard
To: Div. of Parks & Recreation
P.O. Box 1401, Tatnall Bldg.
Dover, DE 19901

HISTORICAL SITES

A state map and a packet of information about the historical sites in Delaware.

Ask for: map and information packet
Send: a postcard
To: Bureau of Museum & Historic Sites
Margaret O'Neill Visitor Ctr.
Court & Federal St.
Dover, DE 19901

Florida

REGIONS

Venice

A guide book to the area around Venice, south of Tam-pa, on the gulf coast of Florida. This booklet relates the history and background of the area and directs tourists to area businesses. Includes a chart of hotels and motels.

Ask for: "Venice Area Chamber of Commerce Guide Book"
Send: 50¢
To: Venice Area Chamber of Commerce
P.O. Box 937GB
Venice, FL 33595

COUNTIES

Charlotte

A directory of shops, businesses and points of interest in Charlotte County, located 100 miles south of Tampa on the gulf coast.

Ask for: "Charlotte County Membership, Shopping & Visitors' Guide"
Send: $1.00
To: Greater Charlotte County Chamber of Commerce
98 Tamiama Tr.
Punta Gorda, FL 33950

CITIES

Fort Lauderdale

- "Gifts of the Sea" (GS), a foldout that describes rec-reation opportunities in Fort Lauderdale and provides a map marking over 150 parks, beaches, recreation areas and attractions.
- "Fort Lauderdale and Lauderdale-by-the-Sea" (AC), a pamphlet that guides visitors to more than 25 hotels and motels and selected attractions.
- "Dining Guide" (DG), a booklet that reviews over 100 restaurants.
- "Marine Guide" (MG), a colorful booklet that includes tips on fishing, a calendar of boating events, a directory of boat yards and businesses, and a summary of Florida boating laws and regulations.

Ask for: each publication you want by name and code
Send: a postcard
To: Fort Lauderdale/Broward County Chamber of Commerce
Tourism/Convention Development
208 S.E. Third Ave.
Ft. Lauderdale, FL 33302

Miami Beach

- "Visitor & Attractions Guide," a pamphlet that directs vacationers to parks, museums, cruises, boat rentals, airlines and many attractions.

FLORIDA

- "Dining Guide," a colorful pamphlet that lists all kinds of area restaurants.
- "Hotel Directory," a pamphlet that includes more than 200 accommodations.
- "Entertainment Bulletin," a brief foldout that is published twice a year and is a calendar for sports events, theater performances and more.

Ask for: each publication you want by name
Send: a postcard
To: Miami Beach Visitor & Convention Authority
555 175th St.
Miami Beach, FL 33139

FOOD & LODGING

A pamphlet that lists almost 400 hotels and motels all over Florida, arranged alphabetically by city.
Ask for: "Hotel & Motel Travelers' Guide"
Send: $1.00
To: Florida Hotel & Motel Assn.—TG
P.O. Box 1529
Tallahassee, FL 32302

A booklet that is a directory of restaurants, hotels and motels in Florida.

Ask for: "Florida Travelers' Guide"
Send: a postcard
To: FL & FSA
Publications Div.
Florida Travelers' Guide
P.O. Box 8871
Jacksonville, FL 32211

PARKS & PUBLIC LANDS

A packet of information for serious hikers and backpackers, including a foldout about the Florida Trail, a fact sheet about the Florida Trail Association and a membership application. If you definitely want to hike the

trail (but don't want to become a member), request an application for an out-of-state permit.
Ask for: tourist information packet
Send: a 9" self-addressed, stamped envelope
To: Florida Trail Assn., Inc.—FS
P.O. Box 13708
Gainesville, FL 32604

CAMPGROUNDS

A pamphlet with a map that lists 180 privately owned campgrounds all over the state. Also includes a packet of foldouts on more than 20 campgrounds.
Ask for: "Florida Camping Directory & Map" and tourist information packet on campgrounds.
Send: a postcard
To: Free Florida Camping Directory & Map
Dept. FS
Florida Campground Assn.
P.O. Box 13355
Tallahassee, FL 32308

ATTRACTIONS

Busch Gardens
A color foldout about the Dark Continent at Busch Gar-

dens, a wildlife park in Tampa. Describes the rides, performances and other entertainments at this attraction.

Ask for: "The Dark Continent, Busch Gardens, Tampa"
Send: a postcard
To: The Dark Continent
P.O. Box 9158
Tampa, FL 33674

Cypress Gardens

A small foldout that describes the things to do at the Cypress Gardens (such as attend their water show) and gives admission hours and directions to get there.

Ask for: "Cypress Gardens"
Send: a 9" self-addressed, stamped envelope
To: Tour & Travel
Florida Cypress Gardens
P.O. Box 1
Cypress Gardens, FL 33880

Marineland

A foldout and a fact sheet about Marineland, an attraction in St. Augustine, in northern Florida.

Ask for: "Marineland" and "Marine Fact Sheet"
Send: a postcard
To: Marineland of Florida
Dept. Z
Rte. 1, Box 122
St. Augustine, FL 32084

Ripley's

- "Souvenir Guide," an illustrated booklet about the Ripley's Believe It or Not Museums.
- "Facts on Time," a booklet of famous facts.
- "St. Augustine Museum," a color foldout about the Ripley's Believe It or Not Museum located in St. Augustine.

Ask for: all 3 publications by name
Send: $1.00
To: Ripley's Museum
P.O. Box 409
19 San Marco Ave.
St. Augustine, FL 32084

Sea World

A color foldout about Sea World in Orlando, located in central Florida. Describes some of the things to see and do at the aquarium, including the "Shark Encounter." Includes a small map.

Ask for: "Sea World of Florida"
Send: a postcard
To: Sea World of Florida, Inc.
Group Sales Dept.
7007 Sea World Dr.
Orlando, FL 32809

Walt Disney World

A large, full-color booklet with all the information you need to plan a trip to Walt Disney World. Includes details on transportation to the attraction, admission prices, special packages and facilities at the complex. Also contains a hotel or campground reservation form.

Ask for: "Walt Disney World Vacation Guide Magazine"
Send: a postcard
To: Walt Disney World Co.
Dept. MP
P.O. Box 40
Lake Buena Vista, FL 32830

Georgia

Seven foldouts suggesting things to see and do in 7 regions of the state. Each publication tells visitors about historical sites, parks, museums and other attractions in that area. Foldouts are available for the following regions:

- the northeast Georgia Mountains;
- Georgia's pioneer territory, in the northwest corner;
- Georgia's plains country, in the southwest corner;
- the colonial coast, in the south;
- the classic South, inland on the eastern border;
- the heart of Georgia; and
- Atlanta.

Ask for: information on any region you are interested in
Send: a postcard
To: Tour Georgia
P.O. Box 1776
Atlanta, GA 30301

GEORGIA

COUNTIES

Wilkes

A packet of information about the town of Washington and the surrounding Wilkes County, located in the northeast part of the state. This area includes more than 40 antebellum mansions, Victorian homes, federal-style houses and original log cabins.

Ask for: tourist information packet
Send: a 9" self-addressed, stamped envelope
To: Wilkes County Chamber
of Commerce
P.O. Box 661
Washington, GA 30673

CITIES

Atlanta

- "Map and Guide," a pamphlet with several maps that introduces you to the Atlanta area.
- "Lodging Guide," a pamphlet with a directory of motels and hotels arranged according to the areas of the city.
- "Dining Guide," a pamphlet that reviews more than 100 restaurants.
- "Calendar of Events," a brief pamphlet that lists festivals, special events, music, dance, theater and sports. Updated every 2 months, so specify the months you are interested in.

Ask for: each publication you want by name
Send: a postcard
To: Atlanta Convention &
Visitors' Bureau
Attn: Tourism/FS
233 Peachtree St.,
Ste. 200
Atlanta, GA 30043

PARKS, PUBLIC LANDS & HISTORICAL SITES

A large color foldout about Georgia's state parks and historical sites. A map of the state marks their locations; a chart shows the activities and facilities.

Ask for: "Georgia State Parks & Historic Sites"
Send: a postcard

To: Georgia Dept. of
Natural Resources
Parks, Recreation &
Historic Sites Div.
270 Washington St.
Atlanta, GA 30334

Atlanta Historical Society

A foldout from the Atlanta Historical Society outlining its activities and describing the historical houses, nature trails, restaurant and shop it manages for visitors.

Ask for: "Historical Society"
Send: a postcard
To: Dir., Public Relations
Atlanta Historical Soc.
P.O. Box 12423
Atlanta, GA 30355

ATTRACTIONS

Six Flags Over Georgia

A color foldout describing some of the rides, shows and activities at Six Flags Atlanta, an amusement park 15 minutes west of downtown Atlanta.

Ask for: brochure
Send: a postcard
To: David Kaplan
Six Flags over Georgia
P.O. Box 43187
Atlanta, GA 30378

Stone Mountain Park

A variety of publications about the 3200-acre Stone Mountain Park, located east of Atlanta.

- "Georgia's Stone Mountain Park," a pamphlet that includes a map and a list of the attractions of the park, which features the largest stone sculpture in the world.
- "Stone Mountain Inn," a pamphlet that describes the park's hotel.
- "The Antebellum Plantation," a pamphlet that describes the park's reproduction of a pre-Civil War plantation.
- "Carving and Geology of Stone Mountain," a pamphlet that discusses the area's rock formations.
- "Family Campground," a fact sheet that lists area campgrounds.
- "Golf," a fact sheet that mentions area golf facilities.
- "Bicycling," a fact sheet that features bike trails.
- "Price Schedule," a pamphlet that lists current prices.

  Ask for: each publication you want by name
  Send: a postcard

To: Stone Mountain Park
P.O. Box 778
Stone Mountain,
GA 30086

Hawaii

- "Hawaii—It's More than a Pretty Place," a foldout with general information about 6 of the islands and what you can do on them.
- "The Aloha State," a pamphlet about the islands' history, geography, economics and more.
- "Golf & Tennis in Hawaii," a foldout about outdoor recreation that describes facilities and lists fees.
- "What to Wear and Buy in Hawaii," a foldout with some useful tips for travelers.

Ask for: all 4 publications by name
Send: a 9" self-addressed, stamped envelope with 3 first-class stamps attached
To: Hawaii Visitors' Bureau
2270 Kalakaua Ave., Ste. 801
Honolulu, HI 96815

REGIONS

The Islands

A set of colorful foldouts about 5 of Hawaii's islands.

Each foldout opens up to display an illustrated map of an island, highlighting beaches, mountains, historical sites, resorts and other points of interest. Distances to other islands are also noted.

- "Hawaii—The Big Island."
- "Kauai—The Garden Isle."
- "Mauai—The Valley Isle."
- "Molokai—The Friendly Isle."
- "Oahu—The Gathering Place."

Ask for: all 5 publications by name
Send: a 9" self-addressed envelope with 4 first-class stamps attached
To: Hawaii Visitors' Bureau
2270 Kalakaua Ave., Ste. 801
Honolulu, HI 96815

FOOD & LODGING

Two pamphlets that list hundreds of hotels, condominiums and restaurants on the islands. Information about rates, facilities and specialties is provided, and addresses and phone numbers are included.

Ask for: "Hotel Guide" and "Restaurant Guide"

IDAHO

Send: a 9" self-addressed envelope with 3 first-class stamps attached
To: Hawaii Visitors' Bureau
2270 Kalakaua Ave., Ste. 801
Honolulu, HI 96815

Idaho

Two publications for the Idaho traveler. One is a booklet that features festivals, national and state parks, museums, campgrounds, ghost towns, ski resorts and other attractions in the state. The second is a large foldout map of the state that highlights outdoor recreation facilities.
Ask for: "Vacation Guide to Idaho" and the "Official Idaho Highway Map"
Send: a postcard
To: Tour Idaho
Rm. 108, Capitol Bldg.
Boise, ID 83720

CITIES

Moscow

A packet of information about the city of Moscow, including a foldout that outlines the city's history and points of interest; a booklet that lists festivals, museums, art galleries and more; brief directories of hotels, motels and restaurants; and a guide to the Dworshak Reservoir Reservation. A state highway map is also included.
Ask for: tourist information packet about Moscow
Send: $1.00
To: Moscow Chamber of Commerce
P.O. Box 8936—FS
Moscow, ID 83843

Stanley

A foldout about the city of Stanley and the nearby Sawtooth Recreation Area. It notes the outdoor activities there, such as cross-country skiing, white-water canoeing, kayaking, snowmobiling and more.
Ask for: "Stanley—Sawtooth Recreation Area"
Send: 30¢
To: Stanley Chamber of Commerce
P.O. Box 45S
Stanley, ID 83278

Twin Falls

A packet of information about the historical sites and natural wonders in Twin Falls, a city on the Snake River in southern Idaho.
Ask for: tourist information packet
Send: a postcard

To: Twin Falls Chamber of Commerce
P.O. Box 123
Twin Falls, ID 83301

PARKS & PUBLIC LANDS

Bureau of Land Management

A number of publications on the recreational use of public lands are available from the Idaho office of the U.S. Bureau of Land Management. Includes information on campgrounds, wildlife refuges, historical sites, and recreation and wilderness areas.
Ask for: information on recreational use of public lands
Send: a postcard
To: U.S. Dept. of the Interior
Bureau of Land Management
Idaho State Office
Box 042, Federal Bldg.
550 W. Fort St.
Boise, ID 83724

State Parks

A colorful pamphlet that includes a state map and a chart of all state park facilities and activities. In addition, if you need more information about a specific state park, list the park; if a publication is available, it will be sent to you.

Ask for: "Idaho State Parks"
Send: 50¢
To: Idaho Parks & Recreation—
Dept. 01
Statehouse Mail
2177 Warm Springs Ave.
Boise, ID 83720

RESORTS & SKI AREAS

Mystic Saddle Ranch

Two foldouts about a ranch that outfits horsepacking trips into the Idaho wilder-ness. Describes 2 available trips and suggests other routes. Includes an area map and a trip reservation form.

Ask for: "Sawtooth Wilderness Pack Trips"
Send: a postcard
To: Mystic Saddle Ranch
P.O. Box F
Stanley, ID 83340

Ski Idaho

A foldout that lists 20 of Idaho's ski resorts, describes their facilities and operating schedules, and explains how to get more information about or make reservations at them.

Ask for: "Ski Idaho"
Send: a postcard
To: Tour Idaho
Rm. 108, Capitol Bldg.
Boise, ID 83720

Sun Valley Resort

A packet of information on the Sun Valley resort, located in central Idaho. Includes foldouts on winter activities, summer recreation and ski trail maps.

Ask for: information on summer and winter activities, ski trails
Send: a postcard
To: Sun Valley Co.
Sun Valley, ID 83353
Attn.: Travel Brochures

Illinois

Two publications about the state of Illinois. One booklet describes hundreds of get-away vacations, festivals, camping and hiking sites, state parks, biking trails, museums and other attractions in the state. Special attention is given to things to do in Chicago. Another publication, a calendar, details what's going on in the worlds of sports, recreation and culture everywhere in Illinois.

Ask for: "The Illinois Weekend Book" and the "Illinois Calendar of Events"
Send: a postcard
To: Illinois Travel
Information Ctr.
208 N. Michigan Ave.
Chicago, IL 60601

CITIES

Chicago

• "Chicago Map & Attractions," a large city map featuring the major hotels, attractions and transportation systems.
• "Entertainment Bulletin," a foldout that lists the monthly events in the city (specify which month you'll be visiting).

- "Chicago Holidays," a foldout that describes dozens of budget weekend packages at hotels and resorts in and near Chicago.
  Ask for: all 3 publications by name
  Send: a 9" self-addressed envelope with 2 first-class stamps attached
  To: Chicago Convention & Tourism Bureau
  McCormick Place on the Lake
  Chicago, IL 60616

LODGING

A comprehensive directory of hundreds of hotels and motels in Illinois that lists the address, phone number and price range of each.
Ask for: "The Illinois Hotel/Motel Directory"
Send: a postcard
To: Illinois Hotel & Motel Assn.
Directory Dept.
P.O. Box 395
Springfield, IL 62705

ATTRACTIONS

Marriott's Great America

Two foldouts with helpful information for the visitor to this attraction in Gurnee (45 minutes north of Chicago).
Ask for: "General Park Brochure" and "Accommodations Directory"
Send: a postcard
To: Visitor Information
Marriott's Great America
P.O. Box 1776
Gurnee, IL 60031

Rockome Gardens

A tabloid newspaper covering the seasonal events and festivals at this theme park in central Illinois. Also features information about the Amish customs that are observed in this park. Maps and a directory of motel and camping accommodations are also provided.
Ask for: "Rockome Gardens Travel Issue"
Send: a postcard
To: Rockome Gardens
Dept. 01
Rte. 2, Box 87
Arcola, IL 61910

MUSEUMS

Art Institute of Chicago

A calendar of events, published 3 times a year, that lists exhibits, plays, lectures and films at the Art Institute. Also gives general information on the institute collection.
Ask for: "The Art Institute of Chicago Tri-Annual Brochure"
Send: a postcard
To: Public Relations Dept.
Art Institute of Chicago
Michigan Ave. at Adams St.
Chicago, IL 60603

Museum of Contemporary Art

A foldout with information on the exhibits, hours and admission prices at this contemporary art museum in Chicago.
Ask for: "The Museum of Contemporary Art Brochure"
Send: a postcard
To: Museum of Contemporary Art
237 E. Ontario St.
Chicago, IL 60611
Attn.: N. Coffin

Museum of Science & Industry

A full-color foldout that describes some of the things to do and see at Chicago's Museum of Science & Industry. Museum hours and a map showing how to get there are also provided.
Ask for: "Museum Color Brochure"
Send: a 9" self-addressed, stamped envelope

To: Public Relations Dept.
Museum of Science
& Industry
57th St. & Lake Shore Dr.
Chicago, IL 60637

Indiana

- "Calendar of Events," published twice a year. Lists each month's festivals, events and important happenings.
- "Indiana Sceni-Circle Drives," a guide to 17 short tours that will take you off the interstate system and onto scenic secondary highways, past historical sites, museums and other attractions.
- "Indiana Industry and Agriculture Tours," a pamphlet about nearly 100 businesses and industries that provide guided tours.

Ask for: each publication you want by name
Send: a postcard
To: Tourism Development Div.—FS
440 N. Meridian St.
Indianapolis, IN 46204

COUNTIES

Monroe

A packet of information about Monroe County and the city of Bloomington, the home of Indiana University. Includes a state map; information about Bloomington, the university and its famous Lily Library; and guides to historical homes, hotels, restaurants, campgrounds and other attractions. A city map is also available upon request.

Ask for: tourist information packet about Monroe County and/or a Bloomington city map
Send: a postcard (information packet); $1.00 (city map)
To: Monroe County Convention & Visitors' Bureau
4201 E. Third St.
Bloomington, IN 47401

CITIES

Indianapolis

- "This Week in Indianapolis" (35¢ and a 9" self-addressed, stamped envelope), a guide to events, exhibits, museums, dining, entertainment, hotels and motels, transportation and more.
- "Indianapolis Presents the Entertaining City, Enjoyably" (free), a foldout describing the city's sights and attractions.

- "Eagle Creek Park and Nature Preserve" (free), a foldout map and directory to the largest city park in the United States.

Ask for: each publication you want by name
Send: a postcard for the free publications; the amount specified for any others
To: Tourism Development Div.
Indianapolis Convention & Visitors' Bureau
100 S. Capitol Ave.
Indianapolis, IN 46255

Madison

A foldout map and directory for Madison, a town on the Ohio River in southern Indiana. Lists historical houses and other sites, museums, festivals, motels, a winery and much more.

Ask for: "Madison, Indiana Visitor's Guide"
Send: a 9" self-addressed, stamped envelope
To: Madison Area Chamber of Commerce
Heritage Sq.
301 E. Main St.
Madison, IN 47250

CAMPGROUNDS

A comprehensive booklet that describes the facilities and activities at both state and pri-

vate campgrounds and recreation areas in Indiana.
Ask for: "Indiana Camping and Outdoor Recreation Guide"
Send: a postcard
To: Tourism Development Div.—FS
440 N. Meridian St.
Indianapolis, IN 46204

ATTRACTIONS

Three brief publications that describe attractions in and around Indianapolis—a 55-acre, open-air museum that recreates life in 1836 on the prairie, a motor speedway hall of fame, and a zoo.
Ask for: "Conner Prairie Pioneer Settlement," "Indianapolis Motor Speedway Hall of Fame Museum" and "Indianapolis Zoo"
Send: a postcard
To: Tourism Development Div.
Indianapolis Convention & Visitors' Bureau
100 S. Capitol Ave.
Indianapolis, IN 46255

MUSEUMS

Children's Museum

A foldout about the Children's Museum in Indian-apolis, the largest museum of its kind in the world. Describes the museum's exhibits and provides a map and information on hours and admission.
Ask for: "Experience the World's Largest Children's Museum"
Send: a 9" self-addressed, stamped envelope
To: The Children's Museum
3000 N. Meridian St.
Box 88126
Indianapolis, IN 46208

Indianapolis Museum of Art

A brief color foldout that describes some of the exhibits and pavilions at the museum. Includes information on admission, hours and tours.
Ask for: "Indianapolis Museum of Art: Make the Most of Us"
Send: a postcard
To: Tourism Development Div.
Indianapolis Convention & Visitors' Bureau
100 S. Capitol Ave.
Indianapolis, IN 46255

Iowa

A packet of information about the state of Iowa. Specify the activities or geographical areas in which you are interested; if a publication on that topic is available, it will be sent to you. The publications offer descriptions of attractions, state parks, recreation areas, festivals, campgrounds, historical sites, museums and more.
Ask for: information on activities and geographical areas you are interested in
Send: a postcard
To: Tourism & Travel Div.
Dept. FS
250 Jewett Bldg.
Des Moines, IA 50309

REGIONS

Indian Hills Lake Region

A large color foldout about an 11-county area in Southern Iowa—the Indian Hills Lake Region. Describes historical places, parks and other points of interest. A map shows visitors how to find these sites.
Ask for: "Indian Hills Lake Region"
Send: a 9" self-addressed, stamped envelope
To: Indian Hills Lake Region
P.O. Box 923
Ottumwa, IA 52501

Quad Cities

Six publications about the Quad Cities area, located on the Mississippi River between Iowa and Illinois. Includes information on Bettendorf, Davenport, East Moline and Rock Island.

- "Iowa's Great Rivers Region," a booklet on festivals, historical sites and other points of interest in Iowa's southeastern counties.
- "Things to See and Do," a foldout about museums, parks, historical sites and attractions in Davenport.
- "Leisure Environments," a foldout about the parks and recreation areas in Davenport.
- "Quad Cities USA," a map and directory to attractions in the area.
- "Quad Cities USA This Summer," a calendar of local festivals.
- "Church Directory," a brief foldout on area churches.

Ask for: each publication you want by name
Send: a postcard
To: Barbara Fox, Mgr.
Davenport Convention Bureau
404 Main St.
Davenport, IA 52807

CITIES

Burlington
A booklet of general informa-tion about Burlington, a town on the Mississippi River. Includes a map plus an 8"x10" color picture of a city park overlooking the river.

Ask for: city brochure and "Mosquito Park" picture
Send: 90¢
To: Burlington Area Chamber of Commerce
807 Jefferson St.
Burlington, IA 52601

Des Moines
Three publications about Des Moines, the capital city of Iowa.

- "Des Moines' Centers of Interest," a booklet with a map of 7 historical, cultural and scientific points of interest, including the Living History Farms.
- "Des Moines' Guide to Hotels/Motels," a booklet on area accommodations. Includes a map.
- "Where to Go and What to Do," a calendar of festivals, concerts, theater, sports and more.

Ask for: each publication you want by name
Send: a postcard
To: Des Moines Convention & Visitors' Bureau
800 High St.
Des Moines, IA 50307

Dubuque
- "Visitor's Directory," a guide to all kinds of area attractions—historical buildings, tours, cultural events, parks, recreation areas, campgrounds, restaurants, hotels and motels.
- "Let Dubuque Call Your Bluff," a color foldout that describes the city's picturesque sights.

- "A Brief History of Dubuque," a foldout.
- "Dubuque Street Map."
- "List of Hotels and Motels."
- "List of Restaurants."

Ask for: each publication you want by name
Send: a postcard

KANSAS/KENTUCKY

To: Dubuque Area Chamber
of Commerce
880 Locust St.
Dubuque, IA 52001

Kansas

Two publications for the traveler to Kansas. One is a large, full-color booklet full of historical background, maps and directories to state parks, historical sites and other points of interest. The other booklet lists hundreds of festivals, rodeos, fairs, art and craft shows, theater productions and other events.
Ask for: "Kansas Travel Guide" and "Calendar of Events"
Send: a postcard
To: Kansas Dept. of
Economic Development
Travel Div., K–134
503 Kansas Ave., 6th Fl.
Topeka, KS 66603

CITIES

Atchison

A packet of general information for visitors to this city in northeastern Kansas. Also includes information on the whole area.
Ask for: tourist information packet
Send: a 9" self-addressed, stamped envelope

To: Tourism Coordinator
Atchison Area Chamber
of Commerce
P.O. Box 126
104 N. Sixth St.
Atchison, KS 66002

PARKS & PUBLIC LANDS

State Parks

A foldout map and directory to the Kansas state parks. Describes each park, explains the rules and regulations, and lists the available facilities and activities.
Ask for: "Your Guide to Kansas"
Send: a postcard
To: Kansas State Park & Resources Authority
P.O. Box 977
Topeka, KS 66601

CAMPGROUNDS

A colorful foldout guide to state and private campgrounds, parks, fishing lakes and recreation areas throughout the state. Includes a map plus descriptions of the facilities available at each site.

Ask for: "Kansas Camping Guide to the Land of Ah's"
Send: a postcard
To: Kansas Dept. of
Economic Development
Travel Div., K–134
503 Kansas Ave., 6th Fl.
Topeka, KS 66603

ATTRACTIONS

Historic Wichita

A brief foldout about Cowtown, a museum that recreates the western town of Wichita as it was in the 19th century.
Ask for: "Historic Wichita"
Send: a postcard
To: Kansas Dept. of
Economic Development
Travel Div., K–134
503 Kansas Ave., 6th Fl.
Topeka, KS 66603

Kentucky

- "Kentucky Travel Guide," a booklet that lists hundreds of historical sites, parks, museums, festivals, fairs, caves and more. Arranged according to 4 areas of the state, it is also indexed by subject area.
- "Kentucky," a foldout describing things to see and do across the state.

- "Kentucky Scenic and Historic Tours," a booklet that suggests 9 tours to take in your own car for an interesting Kentucky vacation. Describes the historical sites and other points of interest on each tour.
- "Calendar of Events," a pamphlet published twice a year.
- "Official Kentucky Highway and Parkway Map."

Ask for: each publication you want by name
Send: a postcard
To: Kentucky Dept. of Tourism
Fort Boone Plaza,
MP–80–81
Frankfort, KY 40601
Attn.: Lilian Lightfoot

CITIES

Louisville

- "Guide to Louisville," a foldout map and guide to museums, bourbon distilleries, historical homes, attractions, river cruises and much more.
- "Louisville Makes the Good Times Better," a general color foldout about the city.

- "Calendar of Events," a periodically published list of theater productions, music, festivals, fairs, sports and art exhibits.
- "Louisville Horses," a foldout about horse breeds, which also includes schedules for area horse shows and information about the Kentucky Derby.

Ask for: each publication you want by name
Send: a postcard
To: Louisville Visitors' Bureau
Dept. FS
Founders Sq.
Fifth & Muhammad Ali Blvd.
Louisville, KY 40202

PARKS & PUBLIC LANDS

Mammoth Cave National Park

A color foldout about this park, located in south-central Kentucky, and its 200-mile network of caverns.

Ask for: "Mammoth Cave National Park"
Send: a postcard
To: Kentucky Dept. of Tourism
Fort Boone Plaza,
MP–80–81
Frankfort, KY 40601
Attn.: Lilian Lightfoot

State Parks

- "Kentucky State Parks," a large color foldout describing 48 state and national parks in Kentucky, with a chart of the available facilities and activities.
- "Rates and Reservation Information," a foldout listing the rates for lodge rooms, cottages and campgrounds in Kentucky's state parks.
- "Special Events Brochure," a calendar of folk and music festivals, arts and crafts shows and much more.

In addition, if you want more information, specify the parks you are interested in.

Ask for: each publication you want by name
Send: a postcard
To: Travel
Frankfort, KY 40601

CAMPGROUNDS

A pamphlet that lists state and private campgrounds throughout 4 regions of Kentucky. Includes details about the number of sites and the facilities available at each campground.

Ask for: "Camping Guide"

LOUISIANA

MUSEUMS

A short foldout that describes 16 museums in Louisville, including the American Saddle Horse Museum, the Kentucky Downs Museum at Churchill Downs and the Museum of Natural History and Science.

Ask for: "Louisville Museums"
Send: a postcard

Louisiana

A full-color booklet that describes hundreds of attractions, historical buildings, museums, festivals, boating trips and public recreation areas in the state. Devotes special attention to activities in New Orleans. Plus a detailed state highway map with inserts of several major cities.

Ask for: "A Traveler's Guide to Louisiana" and "Louisiana Highway Map"
Send: a postcard
To: Louisiana Office of Tourism
Dept. FST
P.O. Box 44291
Baton Rouge, LA 70804

CITIES

Shreveport-Bossier

A comprehensive packet of information about Shreveport and Bossier City, twin cities on the Red River in northern Louisiana. Provides helpful tips on accommodations and describes local attractions, such as the American Rose Center, several art museums, a nature park and more than a dozen lakes. Several city maps are also included.

Ask for: tourist information packet
Send: a postcard
To: Shreveport-Bossier Convention & Tourist Bureau
629 Spring St.
P.O. Box 1761
Shreveport, LA 71166

LODGING

A foldout of information about the rates and facilities of hundreds of hotels and motels in Louisiana. Each entry lists the hotel or motel's address, phone number, price range and special features.

Ask for: "As You Discover Louisiana, Be Our Guest"
Send: a postcard
To: Louisiana Hotel-Motel Assn.
Ste. 1–A
3973 Sherwood Forest Blvd. S
Baton Rouge, LA 70816

HISTORICAL SITES

Hermann-Grima House

A colorful foldout on this National Historic Landmark,

located in the heart of the "Vieux Carre" in New Orleans. The house was built in 1831 and later restored to reflect the "Golden Age" of the city. Guided tours and cooking demonstrations are available daily.

Ask for: "Hermann-Grima Historic House"
Send: a 9" self-addressed, stamped envelope
To: Hermann-Grima House Brochure Requests Dept. 820 St. Louis St. New Orleans, LA 70112

Maine

- "Maine Invites You," a comprehensive booklet describing accommodations and vacation plans throughout the state. Includes many regional maps and a brief calendar of events.
- "Maine Guide to Auto Touring," a pamphlet describing 21 motor tours of various areas of Maine.
- "Calendar of Events," a colorful foldout of major events across the state. Updated quarterly.
- "Maine Guide to Hunting," a helpful booklet filled with information about hunting seasons, license fees and accommodations for hunt-

ers. Includes articles with specific hunting tips.
- "Maine Guide to Fishing," a foldout containing information about license fees, fishing seasons and convenient accommodations.
- "Maine Highway Map," a detailed map of the state.
- "Maine Fall Foliage," a foldout on 11 scenic day trips recommended for the best viewing of Maine's fall foliage. Complete directions and a small map are provided.

Ask for: each publication you want by name
Send: a postcard
To: Maine Publicity Bureau Dept. MPF 97 Winthrop St. Hallowell, ME 04347

CITIES

Bar Harbor

A colorful booklet that offers information on the town of Bar Harbor, located on Mt. Desert Island, off the southern coast of Maine. Includes lists of accommodations, historical sites, attractions, recreation areas and major events. Also provides information on the nearby Acadia National Park.

Ask for: "Bar Harbor Guide Book"
Send: a postcard
To: Bar Harbor Chamber of Commerce P.O. Box FST Bar Harbor, ME 04609

PARKS & PUBLIC LANDS

State Parks & Recreation

- "Maine State Parks," a foldout with information on the state park system. Includes a list of facilities and provides directions to each park.
- "Maine Canoeing," a foldout that provides tips on how to prepare for your canoe trip. Also supplies a list of popular canoeable waters (graded by difficulty) and a guide to helpful publications.
- "Allagash Wilderness Waterway," a packet of information on this 92-mile ribbon of lakes, ponds, rivers and streams in northern Maine. Includes a map, a list of guide and flying services and official regulations.

- "Baxter State Park," a foldout on this wilderness area of 200,000 acres in northern Maine. Provides general information and a map of the area.

Ask for: each publication you want by name
Send: a postcard
To: Maine Dept. of Conservation
Bureau of Parks & Recreation
State House Sta. #19, Harlow Bldg.
Augusta, ME 04333

CAMPGROUNDS

A detailed pamphlet that lists hundreds of camping areas in the state. Lists facilities at each. A map shows locations.

Ask for: "Maine Guide to Camping"
Send: a postcard
To: Maine Publicity Bureau
Dept. MPF
97 Winthrop St.
Hallowell, ME 04347

SKI AREAS

Sugarloaf

A packet of information on Sugarloaf/USA, Maine's largest ski area, located near the Carrabasset Valley in west-central Maine. Includes a description of the area's facilities, ski school and accommodations. Also provides a trail map.

Ask for: information on Sugarloaf/USA
Send: a 9" self-addressed envelope with 2 first-class stamps attached
To: Sugarloaf/USA
Dept. CC
Carrabasset Valley
Kingfield, ME 04947

MUSEUMS & HISTORICAL SITES

A booklet featuring descriptions of historical homes, museums, churches, libraries, schools and other historical sites. Provides an address, admission price and hours for each, plus brief historical background information.

Ask for: "Maine Guide to Museums & Historic Homes"
Send: a postcard
To: Maine Publicity Bureau
Dept. MPF
97 Winthrop St.
Hallowell, ME 04347

A foldout that lists more than a dozen memorials and historical sites owned by the state. Includes a general description and the location of each.

Ask for: "Maine Historic Memorials"
Send: a postcard
To: Maine Dept. of Conservation
Bureau of Parks & Recreation
State House Sta. #19, Harlow Bldg.
Augusta, ME 04333

FESTIVALS

Bean Hole Bean Festival

A foldout that describes an annual festival in Oxford Hills devoted to the old-fashioned method of cooking beans underground in cast-iron kettles.

Ask for: "Bean Hole Bean Festival"
Send: a postcard
To: Oxford Hills Chamber of Commerce
P.O. Box 268
Norway, ME 04268

Maryland

- "Maryland Travel Kit," a comprehensive packet of publications that includes a description of 10 tours of the state, a poster, a state map, a list of hundreds of accommodations and a calendar of events.

- "Kiddie Kit," a fact sheet that offers information about Maryland in a style that's accessible to children.

Ask for: each publication you want by name
Send: a postcard
To: Maryland Office of
Tourist Development
FST—Tourism
1748 Forest Dr.
Annapolis, MD 21401

CITIES

Baltimore

A colorful packet of publications to help you enjoy your visit to Baltimore, the famous port on Chesapeake Bay. Includes foldouts on restaurants, events and important sites such as museums, historical buildings, markets, parks and gardens. Also provides a large city map.
Ask for: "Inside Baltimore"
Send: a postcard
To: Baltimore Office of
Promotion & Tourism
Dept. FS
110 W. Baltimore St.
Baltimore, MD 21209

PARKS & PUBLIC LANDS

State Parks

A foldout that describes the Maryland state park system and provides a map locating all state parks and forests.
Ask for: "Maryland: The Mountains, the Bay, the Ocean"
Send: a postcard
To: Maryland Office of
Tourist Development
FST—Tourism
1748 Forest Dr.
Annapolis, MD 21401

CAMPGROUNDS

A foldout that lists the location of and the facilities available at campgrounds throughout Maryland.
Ask for: "Campgrounds Directory"
Send: a postcard
To: Maryland Office of
Tourist Development
FST—Tourism
1748 Forest Dr.
Annapolis, MD 21401

Massachusetts

COUNTIES

Berkshire

- "The Berkshires' Vacation Guide," a pamphlet that covers lodging, dining and entertainment. Also points out popular sites for camping and outdoor recreation.
- "Variations on a Theme of Vacations," a colorful foldout featuring a map and a list of museums, festivals, historical sites and natural attractions.
- "Circle Tours: The Berkshires," a large foldout map that describes 6 motor tours of Berkshire County.

Ask for: each publication you want by name
Send: a postcard
To: Berkshire Hills Conference
Dept. FST
20 Elm St.
Pittsfield, MA 01201

CITIES

Boston

Two publications about the city of Boston. One pamphlet

lists accommodations, restaurants, theaters, museums, sporting events, tours and area businesses. The second publication is a foldout calendar (updated monthly) of dance, art and museum exhibits, children's activities, concerts, theater, sports, tours and other events.

Ask for: "Official Guide" and "Boston by Week"
Send: $1.00
To: The Greater Boston Convention & Tourist Bureau
Dept. FST
Prudential Tower, Ste. 1944
P.O. Box 490
Boston, MA 02199

PARKS & PUBLIC LANDS

State Parks

A large foldout that lists the Massachusetts state forests, parks, reservations, rinks and pools. Describes the recreational opportunities at each location. Includes a map of the state with the parks and forests marked.

Ask for: "Massachusetts Forests and Parks"
Send: a 9" self-addressed, stamped envelope
To: Dept. of Environmental Management
Div. of Forests & Parks
100 Cambridge St., 19th Fl.
Boston, MA 02202

CAMPGROUNDS

A large foldout, organized by geographical region, showing campgrounds throughout the state. A chart tells what services, supplies and recreational activities are available at each site.

Ask for: "Massachusetts Campground Guide"
Send: a 9" self-addressed, stamped envelope

To: Massachusetts Assn. of Campground Owners
Dept. MP
200 Hillside Rd.
Westfield, MA 01085

SKI AREAS

The Berkshires

A colorful booklet that offers information on downhill and cross-country ski areas in western Massachusetts. Includes a map plus a list of restaurants and accommodations in the area.

Ask for: "Ski and Stay: The Berkshires"
Send: a postcard
To: Berkshire Hills Conference
Dept. FST
20 Elm St.
Pittsfield, MA 01201

Berkshire East Ski Area

A packet of information about the Berkshire East Ski Area. Includes foldouts about the facilities and various vacation packages. Also features a detailed trail map and a list of prices for lift tickets.

Ask for: information on the Berkshire East Ski Area
Send: 50¢

To: Berkshire East Ski Area
P.O. Box 0, Dept. A
Charlemont, MA 01339

ATTRACTIONS

Basketball Hall of Fame

A foldout introducing the Naismith Memorial Basketball Hall of Fame in Springfield, a town in south-central Massachusetts. The hall commemorates the beginning of the game in this town and honors basketball's founder, James Naismith.

Ask for: "Basketball Hall of Fame"
Send: a 9" self-addressed, stamped envelope
To: Basketball Hall of Fame
P.O. Box 175T
Highland Sta.
Springfield, MA 01109

New England Aquarium

A color foldout that describes the New England Aquarium and gives directions to this Boston waterfront attraction.

Ask for: "New England Aquarium"
Send: a 9" self-addressed, stamped envelope

To: Community Relations
New England Aquarium
Central Wharf
Boston, MA 02110

MUSEUMS

Children's Museum

A fact sheet with a map that describes exhibits and activities at the Boston Children's Museum.

Ask for: "Boston Children's Museum"
Send: a 9" self-addressed, stamped envelope
To: Children's Museum
Museum Wharf,
300 Congress St.
Boston, MA 02210
Attn.: Public Relations Dept.

Museum of Fine Arts

A foldout about the exhibits at the Museum of Fine Arts in Boston.

Ask for: "Welcome to the Museum of Fine Arts"
Send: a postcard
To: Museum of Fine Arts, Boston
465 Huntington Ave.
Boston, MA 02115

Michigan

Two publications about what to do and what to see in

Michigan. The first, a booklet, highlights natural attractions, outdoor sports, landmarks, historical sites and festivals in the state. It's arranged geographically by region. The second, a pamphlet, is a calendar of festivals, sporting events, hunting seasons, concerts and plays.

Ask for: "Michigan" and "Michigan Calendar of Travel Events"
Send: a postcard
To: Travel Bureau, Michigan
Dept. of Commerce
P.O. Box 30226
Lansing, MI 48909

REGIONS

East Michigan

- "East Michigan Summer Travel Guide," a full-color booklet listing public and private campgrounds, convention facilities, resorts and motels. Describes opportunitites for many summer outdoor activities.
- "East Michigan Spring Sportsmen's Guide," a booklet emphasizing a variety of outdoor activities. Includes bottom contour maps of Lake Huron coastal areas, designed specifically for anglers.

MICHIGAN

- "East Michigan Auto Guide," a pamphlet for the motorist describing lodges, restaurants, campgrounds, stores, marinas, auto-service stores and other tourist-related businesses.
- "East Michigan Golf and Tennis Guide," a colorful foldout with a road map that pinpoints golf courses and tennis courts.

Ask for: each publication you want by name
Send: a postcard
To: East Michigan Tourist Assn.
Log Office Sta.
Bay City, MI 48706

Southeast Michigan

- "Winterfun" ($1.00), a color booklet listing downhill and cross-country ski areas, restaurants, state parks, private campgrounds, snowmobile trails and vacation packages.
- "Summerfun" ($1.00), a color booklet arranged by county and city with general descriptions of landmarks, campgrounds, state parks, museums, festivals and other attractions.
- "Autumn Color Tours" (a 9" self-addressed, stamped envelope), a foldout describing 13 road tours in the Detroit area and highlighting land-

marks, natural features, parks and recreation areas.
- "Southeast Michigan Outdoor Guide" (50¢), a booklet covering canoeing, camping, boating, hunting and fishing. Includes descriptions of state recreation areas, boat-launching sites and marinas.
- "Accommodations and Attractions in Southeast Michigan" (50¢), a pamphlet that lists hotels, motels, restaurants and other services and attractions by county.

Ask for: each publication you want by name
Send: whatever is specified for each publication
To: Southeast Michigan Travel & Tourist Assn.
American Center Bldg., Ste. 350
Southfield, MI 48034

COUNTIES

Iron

Two publications about Iron County, located in the south-central Upper Peninsula. The large foldout map includes lists of state, township, county, municipal, federal and

private campgrounds. Also features detailed highway routes. The fact sheet provides information about area hotels, motels, restaurants, parks, antique dealers, museums, points of interest, churches, emergency numbers, resorts and cottages.

Ask for: "Iron County" and "Iron County Visitors' Guide"
Send: a 9" self-addressed envelope with 3 first-class stamps attached
To: Iron County Chamber of Commerce
Crystal Falls Branch Office
P.O. Box 68
Crystal Falls, MI 49920

CITIES

Detroit

A color foldout to guide travelers to sporting events, concerts, dance performances, theater, museums, a zoo and other attractions in Detroit.

Ask for: "The Greater Detroit: Same Place, New Face!"
Send: a 9" self-addressed, stamped envelope
To: Visitor Information Ctr.
SPNF-MP
2 E. Jefferson Ave.
Detroit, MI 48226

PARKS & PUBLIC LANDS

State Parks

A color foldout that shows locations and gives descriptions of 80 state parks. Lists campground facilities, interpretive centers and outdoor activities.

Ask for: "Michigan State Parks"
Send: a postcard
To: Dept. of Natural Resources
Parks Div. Office
P.O. Box 30028
Lansing, MI 48909

RESORTS & SKI AREAS

A pamphlet that provides descriptions and maps of downhill and cross-country ski areas all over the state.

Ask for: "Ski Michigan"
Send: a postcard
To: Travel Bureau, Michigan
Dept. of Commerce
P.O. Box 30226
Lansing, MI 48909

Boyne USA

- "Boyne Mountain," a colorful foldout of general information about this ski resort.
- *Boyne USA News,* a tabloid on the events and activities at the resort. Printed twice a year.
- "Boyne Highlands," a foldout about the northernmost peak at this resort.
- "Boyne Nordican," a colorful foldout that describes a cross-country Nordic ski resort on Boyne Mountain.

Ask for: each publication you want by name
Send: a postcard
To: Boyne Mountain
Boyne Falls, MI 49713

Indianhead Mountain Resort

A color foldout about downhill skiing and other recreation at Indianhead Mountain Resort in Wakefield, in the western Upper Peninsula. Includes information about package deals, lodging and dining in both winter and summer.

Ask for: "Indianhead Ski Trip Guide"
Send: a postcard
To: Indianhead Mountain Resort
Rm. 551
Wakefield, MI 49968

Ski Brule

A colorful foldout that includes a price list and general information about special events and facilities at this downhill ski resort.

Ask for: "Ski Brule"
Send: a 9" self-addressed, stamped envelope
To: Iron County Chamber
of Commerce
Crystal Falls Branch Office
P.O. Box 68
Crystal Falls, MI 49920

MUSEUMS

Henry Ford Museum

A color foldout describing Greenfield Village and the Henry Ford Museum, a 240-acre display of historical buildings, vehicles, machines and other items in Dearborn, near Detroit.

Ask for: "Greenfield Village & Henry Ford Museum"
Send: a postcard
To: Greenfield Village &
Henry Ford Museum
Dept. MMP
Dearborn, MI 48101

Minnesota

- "Vacation Guide," a comprehensive booklet of information about mini-vacations, state parks, historical sites, attractions, recreation areas and cultural activities in Minnesota. Includes several maps and a mileage chart.

- "Fall Color Guide," a colorful foldout of information on foliage tours, fishing and hunting seasons, festivals and special attractions. Includes a map.
- "Calendar of Events," a detailed calendar of major festivals, bazaars, contests, races, parades and other events. Updated seasonally.
- "State Map," an official highway map featuring several detailed maps of major cities.

Ask for: each publication you want by name
Send: a postcard
To: Minnesota Tourist
Information Ctr.
480 Cedar St.
St. Paul, MN 55101

REGIONS

Voyageurland

A colorful booklet of information on this region of northern Minnesota. Describes the many rivers, lakes and forests in this area, including those in Voyageurs National Park. Also offers information on ac-

commodations and events in the city of International Falls, located on the northern border of the state. Provides several maps.

Ask for: "Voyageurland"
Send: a postcard
To: Greater International Falls
Chamber of Commerce
P.O. Box 169F
International Falls,
MN 56649

PARKS & PUBLIC LANDS

State Parks

A detailed booklet of information on Minnesota's state park and recreation system. Includes an explanation of park rules and regulations, a chart of accommodations and activities for each park, a list of recreation trails, a section on canoe and boat routes and a list of state waysides. Individual maps of each state park are also available; you can use this booklet to choose the sites you are most interested in.

Ask for: "Minnesota State Park Guide"
Send: a postcard

To: Minnesota Dept. of
Natural Resources
Div. of State Parks
& Recreation
P.O. Box 39,
Centennial Bldg.
St. Paul, MN 55155

State Trails & Waterways

- "Snowmobile Guide," a foldout that describes more than 150 snowmobile trails and offers a map of their locations. Provides detailed information on several state corridor snowmobile trails.
- "Minnesota State Trail Maps," 7 detailed maps of various areas of Minnesota with state trails for skiing, snowmobiling, hiking, horseback riding and bicycling. Specify the area of the state that you are most interested in.
- "Canoeing Brochure," a colorful foldout of general information on 18 canoe routes in Minnesota.

Ask for: each publication you want by name
Send: a postcard
To: Minnesota Dept. of
Natural Resources
Trails & Waterways Unit
P.O. Box 52, Centennial
Bldg.
St. Paul, MN 55155

CAMPGROUNDS

A colorful booklet that describes the facilities available at and the location of private, municipal, county, state and national park campgrounds throughout Minnesota. Also provides information about boat and canoe routes and canoe outfitters.
Ask for: "Camping Guide"
Send: a postcard
To: Minnesota Tourist
Information Ctr.
480 Cedar St.
St. Paul, MN 55101

RESORTS

A booklet that provides addresses, phone numbers, lists of facilities and general price information for resorts that are members of the Minnesota Resort Association. Organized by general area of the state. A small map is included.
Ask for: "Minnesota Resort Directory"
Send: a postcard
To: Minnesota Resort Assn.
2001 University Ave.—FS
St. Paul, MN 55104

SKI AREAS

A large foldout that offers information on over 200 downhill and cross-country ski areas and trails. Includes a map of locations across the state.
Ask for: "Ski Guide"
Send: a postcard
To: Minnesota Dept. of
Natural Resources
Trails & Waterways Unit
P.O. Box 52, Centennial
Bldg.
St. Paul, MN 55155

ATTRACTIONS

U.S. Hockey Hall of Fame

A colorful foldout about the U.S. Hockey Hall of Fame, located in the town of Eveleth, north of Duluth. This museum honors hockey players, referees, coaches and administrators for their contributions to the sport. Offers several exhibits and short films. The foldout gives directions, summer and winter hours and a list of admission prices.

Ask for: "U.S. Hockey Hall of Fame"
Send: a postcard
To: U.S. Hockey Hall of Fame
P.O. Box 657
Eveleth, MN 55734

HISTORICAL SITES

A packet of assorted foldouts on historical sites operated by the Minnesota Historical Society. These sites include the state capitol, several historical forts and homes, an Indian museum, a burial mound, a lighthouse and an old country store. The publications provide old photographs, descriptions of the times and a listing of hours and admission prices.
Ask for: information packet on historical sites
Send: a postcard
To: Minnesota Historical Soc.
Bldg. 25, Fort Snelling
St. Paul, MN 55111

Mississippi

- "Mississippi Calendar," a comprehensive pamphlet listing more than 200 continuing and special events, including films, plays, fairs, exhibits and concerts. Updated periodically.

MISSISSIPPI

- "Mississippi Official Highway Map," a large foldout showing major roads and highways in the state and in several large cities.
- "Mississippi Golf and Tennis," a color pamphlet with city-by-city descriptions of golf courses and tennis courts.

Ask for: each publication you want by name
Send: a postcard
To: Div. of Tourism
Mississippi Dept. of
Economic Development
P.O. Box 22825MP
Jackson, MS 39205

REGIONS

Gulf Coast

A color pamphlet with 4 suggested tours of southeastern Mississippi. Describes various points on route, such as parks and other natural attractions, historical sites and festivals.

Ask for: "Mississippi Gulf Coast"
Send: a postcard
To: Div. of Tourism
Mississippi Dept. of
Economic Development
P.O. Box 22825MP
Jackson, MS 39205

Northern Mississippi

A color pamphlet describing highway tours that take in state parks, landmarks, historical sites and museums in northern Mississippi.

Ask for: "Mississippi Lakes and Hills"
Send: a postcard
To: Div. of Tourism
Mississippi Dept. of
Economic Development
P.O. Box 22825MP
Jackson, MS 39205

CITIES

Biloxi

A packet of general information about Biloxi, located on the gulf coast. Also available is a city map.

Ask for: information packet on Biloxi and/or city map
Send: a postcard (information packet); $1.00 (city map)
To: Biloxi Chamber of
Commerce
P.O. Drawer CC
Biloxi, MS 39533

LODGING

A pamphlet for travelers that lists hotels and motels by city and includes telephone numbers and descriptions of accommodations.

Ask for: "Mississippi Hotels and Motels"
Send: a postcard
To: Mississippi Hotels & Motels
1375 Kimwood Dr.
Jackson, MS 39211

PARKS & PUBLIC LANDS

Two color foldouts about recreational areas in Mississippi. The first describes floatable rivers and streams and lists access points and outfitters. The second foldout has a chart that indicates the campsites and recreational facilities available at lakes, reservoirs and national forests in the state.

Ask for: "Mississippi Rivers & Streams" and "Mississippi Lakes, Forests & Reservoirs"
Send: a postcard
To: Div. of Tourism
Mississippi Dept. of
Economic Development
P.O. Box 22825MP
Jackson, MS 39205

State Parks

A pamphlet, arranged by geographical area, that briefly describes each of the state's

28 parks and lists the recreational and camping facilities at each.

Ask for: "Mississippi State Parks"
Send: a postcard
To: Div. of Tourism
Mississippi Dept. of
Economic Development
P.O. Box 22825MP
Jackson, MS 39205

MUSEUMS

A long pamphlet, organized by region, that lists art, history and science museums in Mississippi. Gives brief descriptions of each museum as well as the address and hours.

Ask for: "Mississippi Museums"
Send: a postcard
To: Div. of Tourism
Mississippi Dept. of
Economic Development
P.O. Box 22825MP
Jackson, MS 39205

Missouri

- "Missouri Travel Guide," a comprehensive booklet with information on state parks, recreation areas, museums, historical sites, night life, sightseeing, boating, fishing, hunting and guided tours throughout the state.
- "Missouri Fun Calendar," a foldout listing concerts, plays, parades, art exhibits and other events. Updated periodically.
- "Missouri Winery Tours," a foldout describing 16 Missouri vineyards that offer tours.
- "Missouri Driving Tours," a foldout guiding motorists along 15 highway trips through scenic landscapes and historical sites.

Ask for: each publication you want by name
Send: a postcard
To: Missouri Div. of Tourism
Dept. FST
P.O. Box 1055
Jefferson City, MO 65101

CITIES

Florissant

A foldout that summarizes the history of this small city, located 20 miles northwest of St. Louis. Describes 20 historical sites.

Ask for: "Explore Historic Florissant, Missouri"
Send: a 9" self-addressed, stamped envelope

To: Florissant Valley Chamber
of Commerce
1060 Rue Ste. Catherine
Florissant, MO 63031

St. Louis

- "St. Louis Visitors' Guide," a color booklet listing sporting events, landmarks, museums, live entertainment, historical sites, natural attractions, hotels and restaurants.

- "Spirit of St. Louis Road Map," a foldout detailing all the city streets.
- "St. Louis Special Events," a fact sheet listing dates and places for fairs, theater, concerts and festivals for the upcoming year.

Ask for: each publication you want by name
Send: a postcard
To: Convention & Visitors'
Bureau of Greater
St. Louis
1300 Convention Plaza
St. Louis, MO 63103

PARKS, PUBLIC LANDS & HISTORICAL SITES

State Parks

A color foldout describing activities, attractions and locations of 59 state parks and historical sites. The text and a chart tell whether lodging, boating, hiking and fishing are found at each site.
Ask for: "Missouri's State Parks and Historical Sites"
Send: a postcard
To: Missouri Dept. of
Natural Resources
Information/Education Sec.
P.O. Box 176
Jefferson City, MO 65102

Montana

A booklet and a map about the state of Montana. The illustrated booklet locates on the accompanying map many historical sites, state parks, fishing sites and general recreation areas. Also charts a dozen scenic tours for motorists and lists the state's museums, theaters, historical homes, inns and churches.
Ask for: "Last of the Big Time Splendors" and the "Official Montana Highway Map"
Send: a postcard
To: Travel Promotion
Bureau—FSFT
Dept. of Highways
Helena, MT 59601

CITIES

Billings

Two publications about Billings. One foldout maps out a city tour, with key historical and geographical spots highlighted. The other foldout lists the city's hotels, restaurants and campsites.
Ask for: "Let Billings Happen to You" and "Billings Dining and Accommodations Guide"
Send: a 9" self-addressed, stamped envelope
To: Billings Area Convention &
Visitors' Bureau
P.O. Box 2519MP
Billings, MT 59103

Bozeman

- "Bozeman, Montana," a full-color foldout that maps Bozeman and the surrounding country and discusses the seasonal features of the area.
- "Welcome to Bozeman, Montana," a foldout that includes both an area and a city map.
- "Bozeman Area Dining Guide," a concise list of Bozeman's restaurants.
- "Bozeman Area Accommodations Guide," a foldout on the hotels in the Bozeman area.

Ask for: all 4 publications by name
Send: a 9" self-addressed envelope with 2 first-class stamps attached
To: Free Literature
Conventions & Visitors'
Bureau
Bozeman Area Chamber
of Commerce
P.O. Box B
Bozeman, MT 59715

PARKS & PUBLIC LANDS

Bureau of Land Management

Information about recreational opportunities on the many acres of Montana public land managed by the U.S. Bureau of Land Management. Includes a variety of publications on specific sites and the available camping, boating, hiking, fishing and hunting facilities.

Ask for: information on recreational use of public lands
Send: a postcard
To: U.S. Dept. of the Interior
Bureau of Land Management
Montana State Office
Granite Tower
222 N. 32nd St.
P.O. Box 30157
Billings, MT 59107

RESORTS & SKI AREAS

Big Sky

A variety of publications about the Big Sky resort. Includes information on downhill and Nordic skiing, backpacking, spelunking, fishing and golfing. Also describes the accommodations, facilities and ski schools. Specify the season (winter or summer) that you are interested in.

Ask for: information on winter or summer activities
Send: a postcard
To: Big Sky of Montana
P.O. Box 1
Big Sky, MT 59716

Circle 8 Guest Ranch

A foldout picturing life on a dude ranch, complete with information on hiking, swimming, riding, hunting and fishing. An accompanying letter explains the ranch's history, describes the accommodations and lists the rates.

Ask for: information on Circle 8 Guest Ranch
Send: a postcard
To: Allen J. Haas
Circle 8 Guest Ranch
P.O. Box 457M
Choteau, MT 59422

HISTORICAL SITES

Custer Battlefield

Two publications about this famous battle. One is a map of the battle that includes an account of the event and its causes. The other is a foldout about the interpretive events commemorating the battle.

Ask for: "Custer Battlefield: Battle Map" and "Custer Battlefield: Summer Activities"
Send: a 9" self-addressed, stamped envelope
To: Billings Area Convention & Visitors' Bureau
P.O. Box 2519MP
Billings, MT 59103

NEBRASKA

Nebraska

- "Vacation Guide," a colorful booklet describing many events, natural wonders, state parks, historical sites, museums and other attractions in the state. Includes a list of state and federal camping areas.
- "Nebraska Events Table," a yearly calendar of major events such as festivals, fairs, rodeos, concerts and more.

- "State Highway Map," an official state map with an illustrated travel guide to major regions of the state and a directory of state campgrounds.

NEVADA

Ask for: each publication you want by name
Send: a postcard
To: Div. of Travel & Tourism
Dept. of Economic
Development
P.O. Box 94666
Lincoln, NB 68509

HISTORICAL SITES

Five publications from the State Historical Society, covering important historical sites in Nebraska.

- "Visit Historic Nebraska," a comprehensive foldout on State Historical Society museums and historical sites, organized by regions of the state.
- "Neligh Mills Museum," an illustrated foldout describing the last complete 19th-century flour mill in Nebraska.
- "Chimney Rock," a foldout about a celebrated landmark on the Oregon Trail.
- "Neihardt Center," a foldout describing this new center in northeastern Nebraska dedicated to the study of the writings of John G. Neihardt.
- "Home of Senator George W. Norris," an information

sheet about the home of a famous Nebraska senator, the father of the Tennessee Valley Authority.

Ask for: all 5 publications by name
Send: a 9" self-addressed envelope with 2 first-class stamps attached
To: Nebraska State
Historical Soc.
Education Dept.
1500 R St.
Lincoln, NB 68508

Nevada

- "Discover Nevada," a foldout illustrated with historical photographs. Describes attractions, outdoor activities, ghost towns and historical sites across the state. Includes an address that you can write to for information on fishing and hunting licenses.
- "Annual Events in Nevada," a calendar of major events with a small state map.
- "Rock Hunting in Nevada," a foldout on hunting rocks in Nevada hills and deserts. Includes a list of common minerals and gems, a guide to potential sites and a list of Nevada rock hunting clubs.

- "Highway Map," an official map of the state.

Ask for: each publication you want by name
Send: a postcard
To: Nevada Dept. of
Economic Development
Tourism Div., Dept. FS
Capitol Complex
Carson City, NV 89710

PARKS & PUBLIC LANDS

State Parks

A foldout describing all the state parks in Nevada. Provides directions to each park and recommends the best outdoor activities for each site. Includes a simple map of the state.

Ask for: "State Park Guide"
Send: a postcard
To: Nevada Div. of State Parks
Capitol Complex
Carson City, NV 89710

CAMPGROUNDS

A booklet of information on camping sites and their facilities, organized into 6 regions. Contains a section on casino camping.

Ask for: "Camping in Nevada"
Send: a postcard
To: Nevada Dept. of
Economic Development
Tourism Div., Dept. FS
Capitol Complex
Carson City, NV 89710

New Hampshire

REGIONS

Greater Manchester

A foldout that describes attractions and recreational areas in the White Mountains. Lists campgrounds, motels and restaurants in the region.
Ask for: "Vacation Guide to the White Mountains"
Send: a 9" self-addressed, stamped envelope
To: Greater Manchester
Chamber of Commerce
57 Market St.
Manchester, NH 03101
Attn.: Inquiries

SKI AREAS

White Mountains

A full-color pamphlet that describes facilities at 8 ski resorts in the White Mountains. Includes information on weekday ski packages.
Ask for: "Ski the White Mountains"
Send: a 9" self-addressed, stamped envelope
To: Greater Manchester
Chamber of Commerce
Attn.: Inquiries
57 Market St.
Manchester, NH 03101

New Jersey

- "Your Vacation Guide," a booklet arranged by geographical region that lists information on state parks, landmarks, museums, resorts, sporting events, historical sites and many attractions.
- "Calendar of Events," a foldout listing concerts, plays, festivals, museums, exhibits, dance and other events. Updated periodically.
- "Your Beach Guide," a pamphlet that explores the state's Atlantic coast.
- "Boat Basins in New Jersey," a booklet about public and private marinas and their facilities. About 300 listings are arranged by county.

Ask for: each publication you want by name
Send: a postcard

To: Tourism
Box CN 384
Trenton, NJ 08625

CAMPGROUNDS

A large booklet that describes more than 100 private campgrounds, as well as camping facilities at New Jersey state forests, parks and recreation areas.
Ask for: "A Listing of New Jersey Campsites"
Send: a postcard
To: Tourism
Box CN 384
Trenton, NJ 08625

SKI AREAS

A foldout on downhill ski areas with information on locations, slopes, fees, package deals, special days and events, accommodations and instruction.
Ask for: "Ski New Jersey"
Send: a postcard
To: Tourism
Box CN 384
Trenton, NJ 08625

New Mexico

- "Where the Southwest Began," a full-color booklet with information on all areas of the state.
- "Official New Mexico Road Map," a map that covers the state and also lists camping and recreation areas.
- "New Mexico Calendar of Events," a listing of major events in the state.

Ask for: each publication you want by name
Send: a postcard
To: New Mexico Travel
   Div.—C & ID
   Bataan Memorial Bldg.
   Santa Fe, NM 87503

CITIES

Carlsbad

- "Information for Visitors," a foldout with general facts about this city in southeastern New Mexico.
- "Carlsbad City," a foldout with information on accommodations, attractions and more.
- "Carlsbad Caverns National Park," a colorful foldout on this nearby national park.

Ask for: each publication you want by name
Send: a postcard
To: Carlsbad Chamber of
   Commerce—FS
   P.O. Box 910
   Carlsbad, NM 88220

Las Vegas

- "The 8 Seasons of Las Vegas" (free), a foldout on attractions in the city.
- "12 Tours" (free), a foldout about a variety of tours in the area.
- A packet of assorted information for tourists (a 9" self-addressed, stamped envelope).

Ask for: each publication by name and/or tourist information packet
Send: a postcard for the free publications; whatever is specified for the packet
To: Las Vegas/San Miguel
   Tourist Div.
   Chamber of Commerce
   P.O. Box 148
   Las Vegas, NM 87701

Santa Fe

A brochure on the capital of New Mexico, with information on museums, historical sites and cultural attractions in the city.

Ask for: "Santa Fe, The City Different"
Send: a postcard

To: Santa Fe Chamber
   of Commerce
   P.O. Box 1928FSFT
   Santa Fe, NM 87501

PARKS & PUBLIC LANDS

Bureau of Land Management

Information about recreational opportunities on the 13 million acres of public land managed by the U.S. Bureau of Land Management in New Mexico. Lists specific sites and the camping, hiking, canoeing, horseback riding, hunting and fishing facilities available at each.

Ask for: information on recreational use of public lands
Send: a postcard
To: U.S. Dept. of the Interior
   Bureau of Land Management
   New Mexico State Office
   P.O. Box 1449
   Santa Fe, NM 87501

HISTORICAL SITES

Las Vegas

A comprehensive booklet on historical sites in Las Vegas,

which is located on the old
Santa Fe Trail.

Ask for: "Historic Las Vegas"
Send: a postcard
To: Las Vegas/San Miguel
Tourist Div.
Chamber of Commerce
P.O. Box 148
Las Vegas, NM 87701

New York

- "I Love New York Button."
- "I Love New York Bumper Sticker."
- "I Love New York Tourism Map," a map of the entire state with inserts of the major cities. Offers brief descriptions of each of the 10 tourist regions and gives addresses and phone numbers for further information.
- "I Love New York Travel Guide," a large booklet that describes the 10 tourist regions in detail and gives essential information on the museums, historical sites, parks, scenic attractions, ski areas and other recreational facilities.
- "I Love New York Calendar of Events," a foldout that is published biannually and lists all of the festivals, exhibitions and other special events that occur in upstate New York.

- "I Love New York Summer Vacations," a booklet of information on motor-coach tours, fly-drive cruises, camping and resort vacations throughout the state.

- "I Love New York Travel Guide: New York City," a booklet with sections on hotels, restaurants, nightlife, theater, museums, galleries, shops and sights in each of the 5 boroughs. A special section on getting around the city includes bus and subway maps.
- "I Love New York At Night Packages," a booklet of hotel/theater packages for all tastes and pocketbooks.

Ask for: each item you want by name
Send: a postcard
To: Tourism
P.O. Box 992
Latham, NY 12110

REGIONS

Four booklets that feature historical and scenic tours of the 4 regions of New York state. They describe parks, museums and historical sites such as the Schuyler Mansion and Bennington Battlefield.

- Saratoga-Capital District
- Hudson Valley from Albany to Kingston
- Mohawk Valley
- Allegany Region

Ask for: "Guide-Yourself Tour" to 1 or more of the above regions
Send: a postcard
To: State Parks
Albany, NY 12238

Hudson Valley

A booklet about the Hudson Valley between Manhattan and Saratoga Springs. Briefly describes attractions, accommodations, restaurants and special events within this area.

Ask for: "Hudson Valley Travel Companion"
Send: $1.00

To: Hudson Valley Pub. &
Information Ctr.
2 Westchester Plaza
Elmsford, NY 10523

Niagara

A large booklet on the
Greater Niagara Area. De-
scribes attractions, campgrounds, hotels, restaurants,
shops, outdoor recreation and
special events throughout the
region. Also includes maps of
the area.
Ask for: "Greater Niagara Vaca-
tionland Travel Guide"
Send: a postcard
To: Greater Niagara Vacation-
land of the Convention
& Tourism Div.
115 Delaware Ave.
Buffalo, NY 14202

1,000 Islands

- "1,000 Islands," a color
foldout featuring towns
and cities in this area
along the St. Lawrence
River. Suggests a number
of tours of the area.
- "1,000 Islands Summer"
and "1,000 Islands Win-
ter," both of which list
festivals and special events
during these seasons.
- "1,000 Islands Attrac-
tions," a foldout that gives
prices and operating hours
for boat cruises and major
attractions.

- "1,000 Islands Fishing,"
a foldout that describes the
fish common to the area
and fishing regulations on
both sides of the United
States-Canada border.
Ask for: each publication you
want by name
Send: a postcard
To: 1,000 Islands
Dept. Free
P.O. Box 428
Alexandria Bay, NY 13607

COUNTIES

Clinton

A packet of information from
this county just west of Lake
Champlain in the Adiron-
dacks. Features information
on accommodations, restau-
rants, festivals and attrac-
tions. Also includes maps of
Clinton county and the city of
Plattsburgh.
Ask for: information and maps
of Clinton County and Platts-
burgh
Send: a postcard
To: Plattsburgh & Clinton
County Chamber of
Commerce
P.O. Box 310FS
Plattsburgh, NY 12901

Herkimer

A pamphlet that contains information on attractions, ac-

commodations, restaurants
and shopping in this north-
central region of New York
state.
Ask for: "Herkimer County In-
formation Guide"
Send: a postcard
To: Herkimer County
Chamber of Commerce
P.O. Box 25FS
Mohawk, NY 13407

Saratoga

A packet of general information on this county, including
a lodging guide, a map and
several foldouts on antiques
and attractions.
Ask for: tourist information
packet
Send: 50¢
To: Saratoga County
Promotion Committee
Dept. FST-2
126 Woodlawn Ave.
Saratoga Springs, NY 12866

CITIES

Albany

- "Albany, the City in the
Country," a booklet about
the capital of New York.
- "Capital/Saratoga Travel
Guide," a booklet about
museums, historical sites,
festivals, cultural events
and outdoor recreation in
the area.

- "Albany Visitor Services Guide," a booklet listing hotels, restaurants and shops in the city.

Ask for: each publication you want by name
Send: a postcard
To: Albany County Convention & Visitors' Bureau
90 State St., Ste. 200
Albany, NY 12207

New York

The New York City Convention and Visitors' Bureau can offer you information on just about anything you want to know about this city. Specify in your request what areas or activities you would like information on.

- "New York City Visitors' Guide and Map," a pamphlet with brief descriptions of points of interest in each section of New York City. The map is keyed to these attractions.
- "Hotels in New York City," a brief foldout listing selected New York hotels (at all prices) and their rates.
- "New York Restaurant Guide," a pamphlet that groups restaurants according to location and gives information on specialties, prices, accepted credit cards and hours.

- "Visitors' Shopping Guide to New York City," a pamphlet that lists stores where you can buy everything from discount clothes to sculpture.
- "New York Quarterly Calendar of Events," a pamphlet that features theaters, music and dance performances, exhibitions, conventions and free events held in each 3-month period.
- "20 Free Things to Do in New York," a foldout that lists some places and events that are free all the time—and some that are free on specific days.

Ask for: each publication you want by name
Send: a postcard
To: New York Convention & Visitors' Bureau
2 Columbus Circle
New York, NY 10019

Syracuse

Two foldouts about Syracuse. The first is a guide to hotels and motels in the Greater Syracuse area. The second provides a map of the city with hotels and points of interest marked.

Ask for: "Hotel/Motel Accommodations" and "Syracuse Travel Guide"
Send: a postcard

To: Syracuse Convention Bureau
1500 Mony Plaza
Syracuse, NY 13202

PARKS & PUBLIC LANDS

Geology

- "New Mountains from Old Rocks," a foldout that explains how the Adirondacks were formed.
- "Continental Collisions and Ancient Volcanoes," a foldout that discusses the geology of southeastern New York.
- "Gems of New York State," a foldout that maps locations where various gems have been collected.

Ask for: all 3 publications by name
Send: a 9" self-addressed envelope with 2 first-class stamps attached
To: New York Geological Survey Booklet Request, Rm. 3140 CEC
Albany, NY 12230

State Parks

- "Guide to Outdoor Recreation in New York State," a large foldout that lists state parks and forests and the activities possible at each.

NEW YORK

- "Winter Activities in New York State Parks," a foldout describing the state park winter facilities, including historical sites.
- "Cabins in New York State Parks," a foldout listing cabins in the parks and giving information on regulations and reservations. Includes a reservation form.
- "Boat Launching Sites" and "Boating Regulations," 2 foldouts that provide all the information needed for boating in New York.
- "Bike Routes," a series of foldouts on bicycling in New York that give routes in different parts of the state. Specify which part or parts of the state you will be visiting.
- "Snowmobiling in New York State," a large booklet that contains information and maps to guide you through the state trail system. Also available is a foldout on "New York State Snowmobile Rules & Regulations."

Ask for: each publication you want by name
Send: a postcard
To: State Parks
       Albany, NY 12238

CAMPGROUNDS

A large booklet that lists public and private campgrounds all over the state. Gives telephone numbers, daily fees, number of sites and facilities available at each. A grid map helps to locate each campground.
Ask for: "I Love New York Camping"
Send: a postcard
To: Tourism
       P.O. Box 992
       Latham, NY 12110

SKI AREAS

A large booklet that describes facilities at downhill and cross-country ski areas all over the state. Includes detailed information on ski packages at many of these areas.
Ask for: "I Love New York Skiing and Winter Sports"
Send: a postcard
To: Tourism
       P.O. Box 992
       Latham, NY 12110

Big Tupper

A brief foldout describing the downhill and cross-country trails at this resort, along with information on tow, rental and ski school rates and ski packages. Plus a pamphlet listing accommodations and businesses in the area.
Ask for: "Big Tupper Ski Brochure" and "Accommodations and Businesses"
Send: a postcard
To: Big Tupper Ski Area
       P.O. Box 820
       Tupper Lake, NY 12986

Holiday Mountain Ski Area

A trail map of this ski area located near Monticello, about 90 minutes from New York City. Plus a foldout on the mountain coaster ride which operates throughout the summer.
Ask for: "Trail Map" and "Holiday Mountain Coaster"
Send: a 9" self-addressed, stamped envelope
To: Holiday Mountain Ski Area
       Town of Thompson
       P.O. Box 629
       Monticello, NY 12701

Whiteface Mountain Ski Center

Trail maps and information on facilities and rates for 3 mountains in the Adirondacks: Whiteface, Gore and Belleayre. A foldout on summer recreational opportunities on Whiteface is also available.

Ask for: information on summer and winter activites on Whiteface
Send: a postcard
To: New York State Dept. of Environmental Conservation
Whiteface Mt. Ski Ctr.
Wilmington, NY 12997

ATTRACTIONS

National Baseball Hall of Fame

A foldout on the National Baseball Hall of Fame in Cooperstown, located 70 miles west of Albany. Includes information on hours, admission rates and routes to Cooperstown.
Ask for: "National Baseball Hall of Fame"
Send: a postcard
To: Baseball Hall of Fame
Dept. MP
Cooperstown, NY 13326

MUSEUMS

George Eastman House

A foldout on this international museum of photography in Rochester. Gives information on the exhibits, the house itself and the operating hours. Also available is a schedule of the unusual and famous films shown at the museum.
Ask for: "George Eastman House" and "Dryden Theater Series Schedule"
Send: a postcard
To: Public Relations Office—FS
International Museum of Photography at George Eastman House
900 East Ave.
Rochester, NY 14607

Museum of the American Indian

A brief foldout on this museum in New York City devoted to the Indian peoples of North, Central and South America. Gives admission rates, operating hours, floor plans and information on access by public transportation.
Ask for: "Visitor's Guide"
Send: a postcard
To: Museum of the American Indian
Dept. FST
Broadway at 155th St.
New York, NY 10032

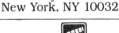

HISTORICAL SITES

A large full-color booklet that describes 26 historical sites in some detail, giving directions and operating hours. Sites include Fort Ontario, Washington's Headquarters and the Walt Whitman homestead.
Ask for: "Exploring New York's Past"
Send: a postcard
To: State Parks
Albany, NY 12238

Old Fort Niagara

A brief foldout that gives a short history of this fort located 20 minutes north of Niagara Falls. Also provides information on admission rates, operating hours and how to get there.
Ask for: "Visit Old Fort Niagara"
Send: a 9" self-addressed, stamped envelope
To: Old Fort Niagara
P.O. Box 169
Youngstown, NY 14174

FESTIVALS

Chautauqua Institution

Several publications from this center for the arts, education, religion and recreation located in Jamestown, 70 miles southwest of Buffalo.
- "Advance Program," a foldout that lists the con-

NORTH CAROLINA

certs, dance and theater performances, operas, lectures and workshops that occur daily through the summer.

- "Visitor's Guide," a foldout that describes the educational, cultural and recreational opportunities available. Gives ticket information.
- "Accommodations Directory," a foldout that provides information on rates and locations for the hotels, guest houses, apartments and houses available during the festival.
- *The Chautauqua*, a newsletter that features articles on performers, programs and courses.

Ask for: each publication you want by name
Send: a postcard
To: Chautauqua Institution
Pub. Office, Dept. FS
Chautauqua, NY 14722

North Carolina

- "North Carolina: Down Home in High Style," a colorful booklet with general descriptions of the state's geographical regions.
- "North Carolina: Calendar of Events," a booklet that covers hundreds of festivals, art exhibits, fairs and sporting events.

- "North Carolina Transportation Map and Guide to Points of Interest," a large color foldout. One side is a state road map; the other lists ski areas, historical sites, outdoor theaters, state parks, national parks and forests.

Ask for: each publication you want by name
Send: a postcard
To: North Carolina Travel
& Tourism Div.
Dept. FS
430 N. Salisbury St.
Raleigh, NC 27611

REGIONS

Cape Fear

A packet of publications for the visitor to Cape Fear Country, a region near Wilmington. Includes information on accommodations, attractions, historical sites, museums, plantations, gardens and more.

Ask for: "Cape Fear Country Vacation Kit"
Send: a postcard
To: Greater Wilmington
Chamber of Commerce
P.O. Box 330
Wilmington, NC 28402

CITIES

Bryson City

A small foldout listing recreational activities, special events and attractions in the area around Bryson City, located near Great Smokey Mountains National Park.

Ask for: "A list of Fun-Filled Activities and Attractions"
Send: a 9" self-addressed, stamped envelope
To: Folkestone Lodge
Rte. 1, P.O. Box 310
Bryson City, NC 28713

Charlotte

- "Charlotte Attractions," a foldout listing historical sites, museums, theater, sporting events and other points of interest in or near Charlotte.
- "Charlotte Hotel-Motel Guide," a foldout with phone numbers, addresses and prices for 28 places to stay in the Charlotte area.
- "Charlotte Major Arteries Map," a foldout showing the major roads leading into Charlotte as well as its downtown streets.

Ask for: each publication you want by name
Send: a postcard
To: Charlotte Chamber of
    Commerce
    Convention/Visitors' Bureau
    P.O. Box 32785
    Charlotte, NC 28232

Raleigh

- "Raleigh: A Capital Idea" (free), a foldout summarizing the history, government, recreation and culture of North Carolina's capital.
- "Calendar of Events" (free), a foldout covering plays, concerts and exhibits. A list of museums, government buildings and parks is included.

- "City and Area Map" ($1.00), a huge foldout with road maps of Raleigh, Wake County and other communities in the area.

Ask for: each publication you want by name
Send: a postcard for the free publications; the amount specified for any others
To: Convention & Visitors'
    Bureau—FST
    Greater Raleigh Chamber
    of Commerce
    P.O. Box 2978
    Raleigh, NC 27602

Winston-Salem

- "Winston-Salem Visitor Attractions," a color foldout describing historical and business tours of this city in north-central North Carolina.
- "Visitor's Guide," a foldout that lists hotels, motels, tours, recreation areas, museums, art exhibits, craft shows, cultural events and other activities.
- "Restaurant Directory," a foldout listing about 70 restaurants in Winston-Salem and the surrounding Forsyth County.

Ask for: each publication you want by name
Send: a postcard

To: Convention and Visitors'
    Bureau
    Winston-Salem Chamber
    of Commerce
    P.O. Box 1408, Dept. MP
    Winston-Salem, NC 27102

LODGING

A comprehensive booklet that lists hundreds of hotels, motels and resorts in the state and describes the facilities and rates of each. Includes a section on country inns.

Ask for: "North Carolina Accommodations Directory"
Send: a postcard
To: North Carolina Travel &
    Tourism Div.
    Dept. FS
    430 N. Salisbury St.
    Raleigh, NC 27611

CAMPGROUNDS

A foldout that describes facilities and activities at 42 private campgrounds and includes a state road map.

Ask for: "North Carolina Campground Directory"
Send: a first-class stamp

To: North Carolina Campground
Owners' Assn.
Rte. 2, P.O. Box 395C
Williamston, NC 27892

North Dakota

A packet of information about
the state of North Dakota. In-
cludes materials about attrac-
tions, museums, historical
sites, campgrounds, recrea-
tion areas, festivals, sports
events and more. Plus maps.
Specify any particular in-
terest you may have.
Ask for: "North Dakota Travel
Packet"
Send: a postcard
To: Tourism Promotion Div.
North Dakota Highway
Dept.—FST
Capitol Grounds
Bismarck, ND 58505

REGIONS

Fargo-Moorhead

A packet of information about
the Fargo-Moorhead (Minnesota) area, including advice
on what to do and see and
where to stay. Also includes
information about recrea-
tional activites.
Ask for: tourist information
packet
Send: a postcard

To: Fargo-Moorhead Convention
& Visitors' Bureau
P.O. Box 404
Fargo, ND 58107

HISTORICAL SITES

A packet of foldouts describing the locations, histories
and facilities of a number of
historical sites all over the
state.
Ask for: tourist information
packet on historical sites
Send: a 9" self-addressed envelope with 2 first-class stamps
attached
To: State Historical Soc.
of North Dakota
North Dakota Heritage Ctr.
Bismarck, ND 58505

Ohio

A large packet of information
to help you make the most of
a trip to Ohio. Frequently includes material on accom-
modations, campgrounds, attractions, museums,
historical sites, special events,
parks and outdoor recreation
opportunities. Specify your
interests.
Ask for: tourist information
packet
Send: a postcard
To: Ohio Office of Travel
P.O. Box 1001
Columbus, OH 43216

CITIES

Cincinnati

- "Cincinnati," a foldout
  with information about the
  city's orchestra, zoo,
  theaters, restaurants and
  other attractions.
- "Cincinnati Restaurant
  and Shopping Guide," a
  pamphlet, divided by
  region and subject, that
  lists restaurants, stores
  and shops.
- "Cincinnati Lodging
  Guide," a foldout that catalogs the city's hotels and
  motels and their rates,
  facilities and phone
  numbers.
- "Cincinnati Downtown
  Map," a foldout with a
  road map and a brief list of
  landmarks and attractions.

Ask for: each publication you
want by name
Send: a postcard
To: Ms. Lois E. Smith
Greater Cincinnati Con-
vention & Visitors'
Bureau—FS
200 W. Fifth St.
Cincinnati, OH 45202

Cleveland

A colorful booklet from the
Convention and Visitors'

Bureau that covers accomodations, amusement areas, performing arts, sports and recreation in Cleveland. Includes several area maps.

Ask for: "Cleveland Visitors' Guide"
Send: a postcard
To: Ms. Sue Shoup
Convention & Visitors' Bureau of Greater Cleveland
1301 E. Sixth St.
Cleveland, OH 44114

Dayton

Two publications about Dayton. One foldout describes area landmarks, museums, universities, parks and other attractions. The other foldout features a map of hotels and motels in the Dayton area.

Ask for: "Discover Dayton" and "Dayton Area Hotel-Motel Guide"
Send: a 9" self-addressed, stamped envelope
To: Ms. Amy Thornton
Dayton-Montgomery County Convention & Visitors' Bureau
1980 Winters Bank Tower
Dayton, OH 45423

Lorain

• "Lakeview Park Rose Garden" (free), a foldout about a city garden with more than 3000 roses of 40 varieties.

• "Greater Lorain Area Motels" (free), a fact sheet listing accommodations in the region.
• "Lorain City Map" ($1.00), a large foldout map of the city.

Ask for: each publication you want by name
Send: a postcard for the free publications; the amount specified for any others
To: The Greater Lorain
Chamber of Commerce
204 Fifth St.
Lorain, OH 44052
Attn.: Tourism

RESORTS

Clay's Park Resort

A color foldout describing campgrounds and fishing and boating facilities at this resort, which has 1000 sites for recreation vehicles. Also a fact sheet about the Yankee Peddler Festival, which features costumed craftsmen.

Ask for: "Clay's Park Resort: The Beautiful Escape" and "The Yankee Peddler Festival"
Send: a postcard
To: Clay's Park Resort—FS
P.O. Box 182
Canal Fulton, OH 44614

ATTRACTIONS

Cedar Point

A color card describing the 57 rides, the campground for recreational vehicles and other facilities at the 364-acre Cedar Point Amusement Park in Sandusky in northern Ohio.

Ask for: "The Amazement Park: Cedar Point"
Send: a postcard
To: Marketing Dept.—FST
Cedar Point Inc.
C.N. 5006
Sandusky, OH 44870

Geauga Lake

A color foldout about the 51 rides, side shows and other attractions at Geauga Lake, an amusement park in Aurora, located between Cleveland and Akron. Lists nearby accommodations.

Ask for: "Geauga Lake"
Send: a postcard
To: Geauga Lake Park
1060 Aurora Rd.
Aurora, OH 44202
Attn.: Public Relations Dept.—FS

Kings Island

A packet full of information about this entertainment complex, located 20 miles north of Cincinnati, that offers rides, attractions and live shows, and hosts the College Football Hall of Fame. Includes a calendar of events, a directory of campgrounds, plus information on other things to do and see in Cincinnati.

Ask for: tourist information packet about Kings Island
Send: a postcard
To: Information Ctr.
Kings Island
Kings Island, OH 45034

Pro Football Hall of Fame

A foldout summarizing the exhibits at the Pro Football Hall of Fame in Canton, south of Cleveland. Includes information on admission prices and hours.

Ask for: "Pro Football Hall of Fame"
Send: a postcard
To: Pro Football Hall of Fame
2121 Harrison Ave. NW
Canton, OH 44708

Roscoe Village

- "Roscoe Village," a foldout describing this village that recreates an 1830 Ohio and Erie Canal town. It is run as a year-round vacation site in downtown Coshocton in eastern Ohio.
- "Roscoe Village Calendar of Events," a fact sheet list-

ing festivals and other events in the village.
- "Monticello II Canal Boat Schedule," a fact sheet with dates and rates of canal tours at the village.

Ask for: each publication you want by name
Send: a 9" self-addressed, stamped envelope
To: Roscoe Village Foundation
Dept. FS
381 Hill St.
Coshocton, OH 43812

Oklahoma

- "Oklahoma!" a booklet with much general information about the state.
- "Oklahoma's Great Outdoors," a booklet on camping, lakes and resorts.
- "Oklahoma Highway Map."

Ask for: each publication you want by name
Send: a postcard
To: Literature Distribution Ctr.
Oklahoma Tourism & Recreation Dept.
215 N.E. 28th St.
Oklahoma City, OK 73105

CITIES

Oklahoma City

- "Saddle Up to a Spirited City," a foldout with map.

It introduces travelers to the sports, museums, theater, other entertainment and attractions in Oklahoma City.
- "Oklahoma City Street Map," a foldout road map with an index to streets in Oklahoma City.
- "Calendar of Events," a foldout listing everything from fairs to festivals, ice shows to films and opera to hockey games.

Ask for: all 3 publications by name
Send: a 9" self-addressed envelope with 4 first-class stamps attached
To: Tourist Information
Oklahoma City Convention-Tourism Div.
4 Santa Fe Plaza
Oklahoma City, OK 73102

ATTRACTIONS

National Cowboy Hall of Fame

A foldout on the variety of cowboy, Indian and settlement lore presented at the National Cowboy Hall of Fame in Oklahoma City. Includes details on admission prices and hours.

Ask for: "Meet the West"

OREGON

Send: a 9" self-addressed, stamped envelope
To: Ms. Marsi Thompson
National Cowboy
Hall of Fame
1700 N.E. 63rd St.
Oklahoma City, OK 73111

Oregon

A large, full-color booklet about the state of Oregon. Describes attractions, activities and historical sites in each of Oregon's 7 regions, with detailed maps. Lists resorts, ski areas, wine tours, golf courses and other points of interest. A calendar of events is also available.
Ask for: "Discover Surprising Oregon" and "Oregon Events"

Send: a postcard
To: Travel Information
Rm. 101–C, Transportation Bldg.
Salem, OR 97310

COUNTIES

Klamath

A foldout guide to year-round recreational opportunities and points of interest in Klamath County. Lists state parks and museums in the area and gives information about Crater Lake National Park.
Ask for: "Klamath Country—Gateway to Crater Lake"
Send: a postcard
To: Klamath County Visitors' & Convention Bureau
125 N. Eighth St.
Klamath Falls, OR 97601

CITIES

Ashland

A packet of publications about the Ashland area, including information on accommodations, historical sites and the Oregon Shakespeare Festival, which is held yearly in Ashland.

Ask for: tourist information packet
Send: a 9" self-addressed, stamped envelope
To: Ashland Chamber of Commerce
P.O. Box 606
Ashland, OR 97520

Portland

A map of the greater Portland area and a full-color foldout featuring points of interest in the city.
Ask for: "Portland, Oregon—Famous for Hospitality, Beauty, Roses" and "Greater Portland Area Map"
Send: a first-class stamp for each publication requested
To: Greater Portland Convention & Visitors' Assn.
26 S.W. Salmon
Portland, OR 97204

LODGING

A directory of motels, motor hotels, resorts and recreational vehicle parks in Oregon. Organized by city, the directory provides the address, phone number and price range of each motel, and describes the facilities. Also includes a foldout map of Oregon.
Ask for: "Oregon's Traveler's Guide"

PENNSYLVANIA

Send: a postcard
To: Oregon Motor Hotel Assn.
12724 S.E. Stark St.
Portland, OR 97233

PARKS & PUBLIC LANDS

Bureau of Land Management

Information about recreational opportunities on land managed by the Oregon office of the U.S. Bureau of Land Management. Lists recreation areas and facilities at each site, as well as information on obtaining hunting, boating and camping permits.

Ask for: information on recreational use of public lands
Send: a postcard
To: U.S. Dept. of the Interior
Bureau of Land Management
Oregon State Office
P.O. Box 2965
729 N.E. Oregon St.
Portland, OR 97208

SKI AREAS

Ski Ashland

A foldout about Mount Ashland, which is located on the Oregon-California border. Gives rates for lifts, the rental shop and the ski school; also provides an operating schedule, a map of the runs and directions for getting there.

Ask for: "Ski the Oregon Challenge at Mt. Ashland"
Send: a postcard
To: Ski Ashland, Inc.
Dept. FST
P.O. Box 220
Ashland, OR 97520

FESTIVALS

Peter Britt Festival

A foldout on the Peter Britt Festival of classical music in Medford. Includes a calendar of events, brief biographies of the performers and ticket information.

Ask for: festival brochure
Send: a 9" self-addressed, stamped envelope
To: Festival Information
Peter Britt Festival Assn.
P.O. Box 1124
Medford, OR 97501

Pennsylvania

- "You've Got a Friend in Pennsylvania," a huge color foldout introducing travelers to the outdoor sports, historical sites, festivals, museums and art exhibits in the state. Includes a state map.
- "Official Transportation Map," a foldout map showing all highways and major roads in the state.
- "Pennsylvania Calendar of Events," a pamphlet listing continuing and special events, including sports competitions, festivals, golf tournaments, art exhibits, plays and concerts.
- "Tourist Promotion Agencies," a fact sheet listing county and city chambers of commerce and travel bureaus. You can contact these organizations for additional travel information.

Ask for: each publication you want by name
Send: a postcard
To: Pennsylvania Bureau of
Travel Development
Box FT
South Office Bldg.
Harrisburg, PA 17120

REGIONS

Pennsylvania Dutch Country

A colorful pamphlet with descriptions of Pennsylvania

Dutch country, located in the southeastern part of the state. Includes sections on antiques, historical attractions, shops, hotels, resorts, campgrounds, farm and tourist homes, tours and guide services. Provides a calendar of events and a detailed map of the area.
Ask for: "Pennsylvania Dutch Country Sampler"
Send: $1.00
To: Pennsylvania Dutch
 Visitors' Bureau
 Box FS
 1799 Hempstead Rd.
 Lancaster, PA 17601

Philadelphia Region
A foldout guiding travelers on 2 motor tours through the region northeast of Philadelphia. Points out museums, state parks, historical sites and other attractions.
Ask for: "Pennsylvania Southeastern Sampler"
Send: a postcard
To: Philadelphia Convention
 & Visitors' Bureau
 1525 John F. Kennedy Blvd.
 Philadelphia, PA 19102

Pittsburgh Region
A foldout describing historical and civic landmarks in Pittsburgh and the surrounding Butler, Allegheny, Beaver, Washington and Greene counties.

Ask for: "Pennsylvania Sampler Trips: Pittsburgh and Neighbors"
Send: a 9" self-addressed, stamped envelope
To: Pittsburgh Convention
 & Visitors' Bureau
 200 Roosevelt Bldg.
 Pittsburgh, PA 15222

Pocono Mountains
A booklet listing ski areas, resorts, golf courses, outfitters, restaurants, campgrounds and other facilities in the Pocono Mountains in northeastern Pennsylvania.
Ask for: "Travel Guide for Pocono People"
Send: a postcard
To: Pocono Mountains
 Vacation Bureau
 Box K
 1004 Main St.
 Stroudsburg, PA 18360

Valley Forge
A large packet of information about the area around this famous site, located just outside of Philadelphia. Generally includes material on accommodations, restaurants, events, museums and historical sites in this region.
Ask for: tourist information packet
Send: a postcard
To: Valley Forge Country Convention & Visitors' Bureau
 P.O. Box 311
 Norristown, PA 19404

COUNTIES

Chester
A color foldout that describes historical sites, architectural landmarks, museums, entertainment, natural and recreation areas and other attractions in this county in southeastern Pennsylvania. Includes a small state map.
Ask for: "Pennsylvania's Chester County Visitor's Guide"
Send: a 9" self-addressed, stamped envelope
To: Chester County
 Tourist Bureau
 P.O. Box 1
 33 W. Market St.
 West Chester, PA 19380

CITIES

Philadelphia
- "Philadelphia," a foldout introducing newcomers to the sights, sounds, restaurants, sports teams and history of the city.
- "Philadelphia in the Fall (or Winter, Spring, Summer)," a calendar of special events, sports events, art exhibits, theater, dance

and music. Also includes a schedule of regular museum shows and a list of city accommodations.

- "Philadelphia Accommodations Directory," a foldout describing hotels and their facilities, locations and rates.
- "Philadelphia Restaurants," a pamphlet that lists city restaurants by the type of food they serve or the entertainment they provide. Includes hours and descriptions of menus.

Ask for: each publication you want by name
Send: a postcard

To: Philadelphia Convention & Visitors' Bureau
1525 John F. Kennedy Blvd.
Philadelphia, PA 19102

Pittsburgh

A large foldout with maps of the downtown and Greater Pittsburgh areas. Also includes a calendar of events listing exhibitions, films, lectures, sports events and dance, music and theater performances. Places of interest and recreation areas in the city are briefly noted as well.

Ask for: "Visitors' Map with Calendar of Events"
Send: a 9" self-addressed, stamped envelope
To: Pittsburgh Convention & Visitors' Bureau
200 Roosevelt Bldg.
Pittsburgh, PA 15222

Scranton

- "You've Got a Friend in Scranton," a foldout that briefly describes the entertainment and activities available in the Scranton area.
- "Hotel, Motel and Restaurant Guide," a booklet listing accommodations and places to eat in or near Scranton.
- "Calendar of Events," a foldout listing concerts, dance performances, tours

and other events in Scranton and Lackawanna County.

Ask for: each publication you want by name
Send: a postcard
To: Visitors' & Convention Bureau
P.O. Box 431
Scranton, PA 18501

York

A foldout and a packet of other information about York. Covers information on geography, history, accommodations, business, banking, housing, media and education. An order form for more publications is included.

Ask for: tourist information packet
Send: 75¢
To: York Area Chamber of Commerce
P.O. Box 1229
York, PA 17405
Attn.: Newcomer's Packet

PARKS & PUBLIC LANDS

State Parks

Two foldouts about activities and facilities at Pennsylvania state parks. The first, a foldout map of the state, shows the locations of 119 parks and provides a description of facilities and a list of rates. Includes a list of outdoor activities. The second foldout includes a map describing ski, snowmobile, equestrian, motor and hiking trails.

Ask for: "Pennsylvania Recreational Guide" and "Pennsylvania Trail Guide"
Send: a postcard
To: Bureau of State Parks
P.O. Box 1467
Harrisburg, PA 17120

ATTRACTIONS

Hershey

- "Hersheypark," a color foldout about the rides, entertainment and exhibits at Hersheypark and ZooAmerica.
- "Hershey for All Seasons," a foldout describing Hershey Gardens, ZooAmerica, Chocolate World and the Hershey Museum of American Life.
- "Hershey Package Plans," a foldout describing a number of package plans that include lodging and admission to Hershey attractions.
- Three colorful foldouts with information about ac-

commodations in the city, including Hotel Hershey, Hershey Lodge and Highmeadow Campground.

Ask for: each publication you want by name and/or information on accommodations
Send: a postcard
To: Hershey Entertainment & Resort Co.
Hershey Information Ctr.
Hershey, PA 17033

HISTORICAL SITES

Gettysburg

A color booklet about historic Gettysburg and its monuments and exhibits. Covers the famous Civil War Battle at this site.

Ask for: "Gettysburg"
Send: a postcard
To: The Gettysburg
Travel Council
Dept. 8C
35 Carlisle St.
Gettysburg, PA 17325

MUSEUMS

Philadelphia Museum of Art

A foldout describing the exhibitions, restaurants, lectures,

tours and other facilities and programs at the Philadelphia Museum of Art.

Ask for: "Philadelphia Museum of Art"
Send: a postcard
To: Public Relations Dept.
Philadelphia Museum of Art
P.O. Box 7646
Philadelphia, PA 19101

Rhode Island

A comprehensive pamphlet that lists recreation areas, points of interest, campgrounds and accommodations all over the state. Includes a calendar of events. Also, if you would like information on a particular interest or event, specify your interest and you will be sent additional material as available.

Ask for: "Guide to Rhode Island" and information on special interests
Send: a postcard
To: Greater Providence Convention & Visitors' Bureau
10 Dorrance St., Box M
Providence, RI 02903

COUNTIES

Newport

- "Tourist Information," a packet that includes

several foldouts covering hotels, restaurants, guided tours of mansions and tours of the city of Newport. A calendar of events is also provided.

- "Visitors' Guide," a booklet that describes the city's museums, historical sites, sailing vessels, mansion tours and other activities.

Ask for: tourist information packet or visitors' guide
Send: a postcard (tourist information packet); $1.00 (visitors' guide)
To: Convention & Visitors'
Bureau
P.O. Box 237FS
10 America's Cup Ave.
Newport, RI 02840

CITIES

Providence

A packet of tourist information on Greater Providence. Includes publications on restaurants, accommodations, attractions and historical sites, as well as a map.

Ask for: "Greater Providence Visitors' Packet"
Send: a postcard
To: Greater Providence Convention & Visitors' Bureau
10 Dorrance St., Box M
Providence, RI 02903

South Carolina

CITIES

Charleston

Two publications about Charleston. The first pamphlet describes tours, museums, galleries, historical landmarks, plantations, recreational facilities, beaches, tennis courts, golf courses, accommodations and places to fish and sail. The calendar of events lists concerts, plays, dances and exhibits.

Ask for: "Vacation Guide to Charleston" and "Calendar of Events"
Send: a postcard
To: Charleston Trident
Chamber of Commerce
Visitor Information Ctr.
P.O. Box 975FS
Charleston, SC 29402

PARKS & PUBLIC LANDS

State Parks

A pamphlet listing the state's 41 parks by region with information about facilities, activities and rates.

Ask for: "South Carolina State Parks"
Send: a postcard
To: South Carolina State Parks
1205 Pendleton St.
Columbia, SC 29201

South Dakota

- "South Dakota Vacation Guide," a booklet with maps. Describes accommodations, campgrounds, hunting, fishing, museums, outdoor programs, auto and horse racing, skiing and snowmobiling. Includes a calendar of fairs, rodeos, art shows and other events.
- "Roam Free in South Dakota," a booklet that emphasizes South Dakota's natural beauty and history, with brief descriptions and many photos.
- "Highway Map," a large foldout map showing highways and major roads.
- "South Dakota Winter," a booklet that describes skiing and snowmobiling in the state.
- "Farming and Ranching South Dakota," a map of ranching and farming areas in the state. Lists agricultural tours and exhibits.

- "South Dakota Lakes and Streams," a color booklet that describes fishing and other recreation in South Dakota waters.
- "South Dakota Rockhound Guide," a foldout explaining the geology of the state. Includes a map showing different formations and the locations of fossils.

Ask for: each publication you want by name
Send: a postcard
To: South Dakota Div.
of Tourism
Dept. MP
221 S. Central
Pierre, SD 57501

CITIES

Rapid City
A packet of information on this city in southwest South Dakota, near the Black Hills. Includes publications on restaurants, hotels, campgrounds, special events and outdoor recreation in the city and surrounding area.

Ask for: tourist information packet
Send: a postcard
To: Rapid City Convention Visitors' Bureau
P.O. Box 747F
Rapid City, SD 57709

REGIONS

Glacial Lakes Region
A foldout about the Glacial Lakes region, with a map providing general information about outdoor activities in northeastern South Dakota.

Ask for: "South Dakota's Glacial Lakes Region"
Send: a postcard
To: South Dakota Glacial Lakes Assn.
P.O. Box 1113
Watertown, SD 57201

FOOD & LODGING

A comprehensive publication, arranged by city, that lists and describes various hotels, motels, campgrounds and restaurants in the state.

Ask for: "South Dakota Hospitality Directory"
Send: a postcard
To: South Dakota Hospitality Assn.
P.O. Box 1580
Rapid City, SD 57709

MUSEUMS & HISTORICAL SITES

A pamphlet outlining South Dakota's history and prehistory—from the age of dinosaurs to the settlement of the state. Gives information on many museums and historical sites all over the state.

Ask for: "South Dakota History and Heritage"
Send: a postcard
To: South Dakota Div.
of Tourism
Dept. MP
221 S. Central
Pierre, SD 57501

TENNESSEE

Tennessee

- "Follow Me to Tennessee," a booklet introducing the newcomer to the cities of Tennessee and to activities like boating, canoeing, fishing, biking and skiing.
- "Fishing in Tennessee," a foldout with a map showing lakes, rivers and reservoirs suited to fishing for bass, walleyes, catfish and other sport fish.
- "Outdoors in Tennessee," a colorful pamphlet about canoeing, kayaking, hiking and other outdoor sports.
- "Events in Tennessee," a calendar of concerts, exhibits, parades, dance performances, plays and other events.

Ask for: each publication you want by name
Send: a postcard
To: Tennessee Tourist
Development
Rm. FS
P.O. Box 23170
Nashville, TN 37202

CITIES

Memphis

- "Memphis Calendar of Events" (50¢), a foldout listing exhibits, concerts, dance performances, films, sports competitions, theater and special events.
- "Memphis Map" (free), a city map that shows points of interest, including galleries, parks, gardens, tours and architectural landmarks.
- "Annual Special Events" (free), a fact sheet that lists many special events and festivals.

Ask for: each publication you want by name
Send: a postcard for the free publications; the amount specified for any others
To: Convention & Visitors'
Bureau of Memphis
Communication Dept.,
Travelers' Services
12 S. Main, Ste. 107
Memphis, TN 38103

PARKS & PUBLIC LANDS

State Parks

Two publications about Tennessee state parks. The first foldout lists all 41 state parks with a brief description of their facilities and activities. The second foldout is a rate sheet for state-owned inns, cabins, group camps, campgrounds, golf courses and other facilities.

Ask for: "TORAS" and "Tennessee State Park Rate Sheet"
Send: a postcard
To: Ms. Faye Buttrey—Park
Information
Tennessee State Parks
2611 W. End Ave.
Nashville, TN 37203

A foldout describing 38 state parks, some with resorts and cabins. A chart lists their recreational facilities and briefly details their highlights.

Ask for: "State Parks in Tennessee"
Send: a postcard
To: Tennessee Tourist
Development
Rm. FS
P.O. Box 23170
Nashville, TN 37202

CAMPGROUNDS

A pamphlet, organized by city, listing public and private campgrounds and primitive camps all over the state. Briefly describes the facilities at each site.

Ask for: "Camping in Tennessee"
Send: a postcard

To: Tennessee Tourist
Development
Rm. FS
P.O. Box 23170
Nashville, TN 37202

ATTRACTIONS

Lost Sea

A packet of assorted publications on the Lost Sea, the world's largest known underground lake, and the nearby Craighead Caverns. Includes information on guided tours and trips on the lake in glass-bottomed boats.

Ask for: tourist information packet
Send: a 9" self-addressed, stamped envelope
To: Lost Sea Inc.
Rte. 2, Lost Sea Pike
Sweetwater, TN 37874

Opryland

A packet of general information about the Opryland entertainment complex in Nashville. Generally includes information on the Opryland U.S.A. musical entertainment theme park, the Grand Ole Opry, the Opryland Hotel and general facts about points of interest in Nashville.

Ask for: tourist information packet
Send: a postcard
To: Opryland Information Ctr.
2802 Opryland Dr.
Nashville, TN 37214

Rock City

A color foldout about tours of the spectacular rock formations on Lookout Mountain near Chattanooga. Includes a map, a list of hours and a description of the facilities.

Ask for: "Rock City"
Send: a postcard
To: Rock City Gardens
Dept. A
1400 Patten Rd.
Lookout Mountain,
TN 37350

Ruby Falls

A color foldout about the 145-foot Ruby Falls and other formations in the caves beneath Lookout Mountain near Chattanooga. Provides a map and a list of hours.

Ask for: "Ruby Falls"
Send: a postcard
To: Ruby Falls
Dept. FT
Rte. 4
Chattanooga, TN 37409

MUSEUMS & HISTORICAL SITES

An extensive pamphlet that describes dozens of historical sites, museums and monuments throughout the state. Features the Davy Crockett Cabin; the Rugby colony, built by Thomas Hughes, author of *Tom Brown's Schooldays*; the Jack Daniels Distillery; and many beautiful mansions.

Ask for: "History in Tennessee"
Send: a postcard
To: Tennessee Tourist
Development
Rm. FS
P.O. Box 23170
Nashville, TN 37202

TEXAS

Texas

- "Texas," a comprehensive booklet of information for the traveler. Includes details on accommodations, campgrounds, attractions, outdoor activities, historical sites, museums, parks and more.
- "Highway Map," an official state map.
- "Calendar of Events," a foldout listing major events across the state.
- "Flowers of Texas," a foldout illustrated with photographs of the state's many species of wildflowers.
- "Texas Rocks and Fossils," a foldout of special interest to rock hounds and collectors.

Ask for: each publication you want by name
Send: a postcard
To: Texas
    Dept. DHT
    P.O. Box 5064
    Austin, TX 78763

COUNTIES

Tyler

A colorful foldout about events, festivals and attractions in Tyler County, in southeast Texas. Includes a description of the "Big Thicket National Preserve," a biological preserve of over 84,000 acres. Also lists accommodations in the area.

Ask for: "Gateway to the Big Thicket"
Send: a 9" self-addressed, stamped envelope
To: Tyler County Chamber
    of Commerce
    Dept. MP
    507 N. Pine St.
    Woodville, TX 75979

CITIES

Austin

A foldout with a map of the capitol complex and descriptions of a number of buildings of historical interest.

Ask for: "Texas Capitol Guide"
Send: a postcard
To: Texas
    Dept. DHT
    P.O. Box 5064
    Austin, TX 78763

Brazosport

A packet of information about Brazosport, a city located on the gulf coast of Texas. Includes a brochure of general information about the area, a fact sheet about "crabbing" (fishing for crabs) and a foldout on fishing in the nearby waters.

Ask for: tourist information packet
Send: a 9" self-addressed envelope with 2 first-class stamps attached
To: Brazosport Visitors'
    & Convention Council
    P.O. Box 2470
    Brazosport, TX 77541

Corpus Christi

- "Area Visitors' Map," a map of this city on the gulf coast and its environs.
- "Texas Tropical Coast," a detailed guide to the coastal area near Corpus Christi. Covers main attractions, festivals, recreation areas, accommodations, shopping and more.
- "Points of Interest," a foldout about significant attractions and historical sites in the area.
- "Where to Stay," a foldout that lists accommodations in the city.
- "Where to Eat," a foldout listing area restaurants.
- "Fishing Guide," a foldout with fishing tips and a map that lists several specific fishing sites.
- "Calendar of Events."

Ask for: each publication you want by name

Send: a postcard
To: Corpus Christi Area Convention & Tourist Bureau
P.O. Box 2664FS
Corpus Christi, TX 78403

Dallas

Two publications about the city of Dallas. The first, a comprehensive pamphlet, includes general information about the city. The second, a fact sheet, lists major events and is updated quarterly.
Ask for: "Dallas Visitors' Guide" and "Dallas Calendar of Events"
Send: a postcard
To: Dallas Chamber of Commerce
Information Dept.
Convention & Visitors' Bureau
1507 Pacific Ave.
Dallas, TX 75201

Del Rio

Two foldouts about the area near Del Rio, a city on the Rio Grande. Provides information on attractions, historical sites, museums and recreation areas. Includes a map of the area.
Ask for: tourist information packet
Send: a postcard
To: Garry W. Kyle
Del Rio Chamber of Commerce
P.O. Box 1388
Del Rio, TX 78840

El Paso

- "El Paso Poster," a colorful poster about this city on the Rio Grande, with illustrations of important sights.
- "Exploring El Paso," a foldout that describes many walking and motoring tours of the city. Also includes a section about the missions in the area.
- "El Paso Sights and Highlights," a foldout about the attractions and historical sites in the city. Provides a city map. Also offers information about a nearby Mexican city, Juarez.

Ask for: each publication you want by name
Send: a postcard
To: Mary M. Ranc
El Paso Convention & Visitors' Bureau
5 Civic Center Plaza
El Paso, TX 79999

Fort Stockton

Two colorful publications about the city of Fort Stockton. The first is a foldout about this community in the "Big Bend Country" of western Texas. Includes general information, many photographs of attractions and a city map. The second publication is a foldout that describes the natural wonders,
outdoor activities and campgrounds in this park.
Ask for: "Fort Stockton" and "Big Bend National Park"
Send: a postcard
To: Fort Stockton Chamber of Commerce
P.O. Box C
Fort Stockton, TX 79735

Fort Worth

- "Touring Fort Worth and Tarrant County," a foldout on local points of interest.
- "Guide to Dining and Entertainment," a foldout that lists restaurants, clubs and entertainment sites in Fort Worth and Tarrant County.
- "City Map," a detailed map of Fort Worth.

Ask for: each publication you want by name
Send: a postcard
To: Fort Worth Convention & Visitors' Bureau
Visitor Information
700 Throckmorton
Fort Worth, TX 76102

Tyler

An assortment of brochures about the city of Tyler, located in eastern Texas. Includes general information about the city, plus specific descriptions of the local Rose Festival, state park and nearby recreation areas.

Ask for: tourist information packet
Send: a postcard
To: Tyler Area Chamber
of Commerce
P.O. Box 390
Tyler, TX 75710

Wharton

A foldout describing this small town in eastern Texas. Offers information on accommodations, local attractions, hunting and fishing areas, museums and local industries.
Ask for: "Wharton, A Small Town Worth Seeing"
Send: a postcard
To: Faye Evans
Wharton Chamber of Commerce & Agriculture
225 N. Richmond Rd.
Wharton, TX 77488

CAMPGROUNDS

A large foldout that lists all the public camping areas in Texas. Describes the facilities and location of each.
Ask for: "Texas Public Campgrounds"
Send: a postcard
To: Texas
Dept. DHT
P.O. Box 5064
Austin, TX 78763

ATTRACTIONS

Six Flags Over Texas

A foldout and a fact sheet about this theme park located in Arlington, midway between Dallas and Fort Worth. Describes the rides, shows and attractions. Also lists the hours and admission prices.
Ask for: general brochure and fact sheet
Send: a postcard
To: Six Flags Over Texas
Dept. FS
P.O. Box 191
Arlington, TX 76010

Utah

- "Utah Travel Guide," a booklet of tips to help the traveler have a terrific vacation in Utah. Includes a calendar of events, facts about the state, a list of accommodations and more.
- "Utah Recreation Guide," a booklet that describes all types of outdoor recreation and provides information about the best areas for specific activities.
- "Utah Story," a foldout that covers many interesting facts about the state, its history and its major attractions.

- "Utah! Best of the West," a glossy booklet filled with beautiful photographs and text about the regions of the state.

Ask for: each publication you want by name
Send: a postcard
To: Utah Travel Council
Dept. MT
Council Hall, Capitol Hill
Salt Lake City, UT 84114

REGIONS

Golden Spike Empire

A full-color booklet on this area in the northwestern corner of Utah. Gives information on parks, campgrounds, and hotels.
Ask for: "Golden Spike Empire Brochure"
Send: a postcard
To: Golden Spike Empire, Inc.
P.O. Box 1601
Ogden, UT 84402

PARKS & PUBLIC LANDS

Bureau of Land Management

A wide variety of publications about use of public lands is

available from the Utah state office. Includes information on birdwatching, natural wonders, camping sites on public lands, recreation sites, motorbike trails, hiking trails, canoeing and other types of outdoor recreation.

Ask for: each publication you want by specific topic or subject area
Send: a postcard
To: U.S. Dept. of the Interior
Bureau of Land Management
Utah State Office
136 E. South Temple
Salt Lake City, UT 84111

National Parks

A foldout about the 5 national parks and 2 national recreation areas located within the state. Gives information on the climate, accommodations, campgrounds, hiking and wildlife in Arches, Bryce Canyon, Canyonlands, Capitol Reef and Zion National Parks.

Ask for: "Utah! National Park State"
Send: a postcard
To: Utah Travel Council
Dept. MT
Council Hall, Capitol Hill
Salt Lake City, UT 84114

SKI AREAS

A comprehensive guide to ski resorts and trails across the state. Describes the facilities at each resort, the lodging available in the area and the ski packages offered.

Ask for: "Utah Ski Planner"
Send: a postcard
To: Utah Travel Council
Dept. MT
Council Hall, Capitol Hill
Salt Lake City, UT 84114

Vermont

- "Vermont Brief" (free), a fact sheet summarizing basic information about the state. Includes a simple state map.

- "Vermont Traveler's Guidebook" ($1.00), a comprehensive pamphlet about attractions, accommodations, camping sites, restaurants and other points of interest all across the state.

- "Vermont Craft Treasure Trails" (50¢), a map and guide to covered bridges, country stores, and craft and antique shops throughout the state.

- "Vermont Summer Map and Guide" (50¢), a detailed map with helpful information on summer events.

Ask for: each publication you want by name
Send: a postcard for the free publication; the amount specified for any others
To: Vermont State Chamber
of Commerce
P.O. Box 37
Montpelier, VT 05602

A wide assortment of publications available from the Vermont Travel Division. Interested travelers should specify the topics they are interested in. Topics include winter ski facts, seasonal events, attractions, state parks, fishing and hunting. A general Vermont vacation guide and an official state map are also available.

VIRGINIA

Ask for: information on specific topics you are interested in
Send: a postcard
To: Vermont Travel Div.
Agency of Development & Community Affairs
Montpelier, VT 05602

CAMPGROUNDS

A detailed foldout from the Vermont Association of Private Campground Owners and Operators. Provides a map of the state with campgrounds clearly marked. Also describes the facilities and location of each campground.
Ask for: directory

Send: a 9" self-addressed, stamped envelope
To: VAPCOO—Ron Wright
c/o Brattleboro North KOA
R.R. 2, Box 110
Putney, VT 05346

SKI AREAS

A large foldout with a map of ski resorts in Vermont and a guide to restaurants and accommodations near ski areas. Many of the hotels and lodges listed are located on extensive cross-country ski trails and offer ski rentals and instruction.
Ask for: "Vermont Ski Map & Guide"
Send: 50¢
To: Vermont State Chamber of Commerce
P.O. Box 37
Montpelier, VT 05602

Virginia

- "Virginia Travel Packet," a packet of publications about the state, including a booklet of general information, an official state highway map and more.
- "Saltwater/Freshwater Fishing," 2 foldouts that describe fishing in Virginia.

Both explain the regulations and provide information on good fishing sites.
- "Golf in Virginia," a foldout that provides information on golfing in the state.

Ask for: each publication you want by name
Send: a postcard
To: Virginia State Travel Service
Dept. FST
6 N. Sixth St.
Richmond, VA 23219

CITIES

Norfolk

A colorful pamphlet about Norfolk. Describes attractions, museums, historical sites, festivals, recreation areas, accommodations and entertainment. Even includes famous local recipes. Also features a detailed map.
Ask for: "Norfolk Visitor's Guide"
Send: a postcard
To: Norfolk Convention & Visitors' Bureau
Dept. FST
Monticello Arcade
Norfolk, VA 23510

Richmond

- "Hotels, Motels in Richmond," a brief foldout listing hotels and their rates and facilities.

- "A Guide to Dining in Richmond," a foldout describing the specialties at many restaurants in town.
- "50 Things to Do and See in Richmond," a foldout about historical sites, museums, attractions and parks in the city and surrounding area.
- "Richmond Map," a map that shows the downtown area and the major arterial roads. Points out major attractions.
- "Richmond Walking Tour," a foldout that outlines a self-guided tour and gives extensive information about the sites on the route.

Ask for: each publication you want by name
Send: a postcard
To: Richmond Convention & Visitors' Bureau
P.O. Box 12324
Richmond, VA 23241
Attn.: CF

Virginia Beach

A packet of general information on Virginia Beach. Includes an extensive directory of accommodations and a foldout on museums, amusement parks, historical sites and festivals in the city.

Ask for: information packet on Virginia Beach vacations

Send: a postcard
To: Virginia Beach Visitors' Bureau
P.O. Box 200
Virginia Beach, VA 23458

FOOD & LODGING

A large pamphlet that gives detailed information on more than 375 hotels, motels and restaurants in the state.

Ask for: "Accommodations in Virginia"
Send: 50¢
To: Virginia Travel Council
P.O. Box 15067
Richmond, VA 23227

PARKS & PUBLIC LANDS

State Parks

A comprehensive booklet that offers information on all Virginia state parks. Provides descriptions of location, facilities, outdoor activities and more. Includes a map of the state showing all major state parks and historical sites.

Ask for: "Virginia State Parks: A Natural Adventure Close to Home"

Send: a postcard
To: Commonwealth of Virginia
Dept. of Conservation & Economic Development
Div. of Parks
1201 Washington Bldg.
Capitol Square
Richmond, VA 23219

CAMPGROUNDS

A large foldout that lists private and public campgrounds in the state and outlines their facilities.

Ask for: "Campgrounds in Virginia"
Send: 25¢
To: Virginia Travel Council
P.O. Box 15067
Richmond, VA 23227

ATTRACTIONS

Wolf Trap

An attractive, full-color poster about Wolf Trap Farm Park for the Performing Arts, located in Vienna, Virginia. Provides a complete calendar of a wide range of summer musical performances on the reverse side of the poster. Includes information on accommodations, concert facilities and ticket prices.

WASHINGTON

Ask for: "Wolf Trap Poster"
Send: a postcard
To: The Wolf Trap
Foundation—MP
Marketing Office
1624 Trap Rd.
Vienna, VA 22180

HISTORICAL SITES

Two foldouts on historical sites in Virginia. The first describes the many famous homes in Virginia, including those of 8 former presidents. The second foldout discusses Virginia's various Civil War sites and battlefields.
Ask for: "Historic Homes in Virginia" and "Virginia's Civil War Battlefield Parks"
Send: a postcard
To: Virginia State Travel Service
Dept. FS
6 N. Sixth St.
Richmond, VA 23219

Washington

A packet of assorted publications about the state of Washington. Brochures may include information on major attractions, recreation areas, state parks, historical sites, museums, cultural events, festivals, accommodations and more. Maps of the state and of specific regions are provided. If you wish to receive information about a particular interest, specify the topic in your request.
Ask for: "Washington State Travel Information Packet"
Send: a postcard
To: Travel Development
Div.—FST
Dept. of Commerce &
Economic Development
Rm. G–3, General
Administration Bldg.
Olympia, WA 98504

REGIONS

Puyallup Valley

A packet of information about the greater Puyallup Valley, an area in western Washington at the foothills of the Cascade Range. Includes brochures on topics such as the local wineries, museums, historical sites and an observatory. Also provides general facts about the area.
Ask for: information on Puyallup and local attractions
Send: a postcard
To: Puyallup Valley Chamber
of Commerce
Linden Village
2823 E. Main
Puyallup, WA 98371

CITIES

Longview

A packet of information on the city of Longview, located 40 air miles from the Mt. St. Helens volcano. Provides facts about the volcano, accommodations, restaurants and local services.
Ask for: tourist information packet
Send: a postcard
To: Longview Chamber
of Commerce
1563 Olympia Way
Longview, WA 98632

PARKS & PUBLIC LANDS

State Parks

A guide to Washington state parks and recreation areas across the state. Includes a description of the location and facilities at each site. This booklet groups these areas into several regions of the state for easy location while traveling.
Ask for: "Washington State Annual Outdoor Recreation Guide"

Send: a 9" self-addressed envelope with 3 first-class stamps attached
To: Washington State Parks & Recreation Comm.
Public Affairs Office
7150 Cleanwater Ln.,
KY–11
Olympia, WA 98504

West Virginia

Two publications about the state of West Virginia. The first, a colorful booklet, is full of helpful facts about state attractions, recreation areas, museums, festivals, fairs, state parks, historical sites and more. Includes a large highway map. The second, a pamphlet, is a detailed listing of major events across the state.
Ask for: "West Virginia Camp Book" and "West Virginia Calendar of Events"
Send: a postcard
To: Travel Development—
GOECD
Bldg. 6, Rm. B–553
Charleston, WV 25305

CITIES

Huntington

An assortment of publications about this city at the junction of the Ohio and Big Sandy rivers. One foldout, "The Huntington Experience," lists restaurants, hotels and shops. Other foldouts describe local attractions, including glass factories, local art galleries, an amusement park and a historic village.
Ask for: "The Huntington Experience" and information on local attractions
Send: a 9" self-addressed envelope with 3 first-class stamps attached
To: Huntington Convention & Visitors' Bureau
P.O. Box 1509
Huntington, WV 25716

Wisconsin

- "Wisconsin Annual Events," a large pamphlet listing festivals, fairs, races and other special events held throughout the year in Wisconsin.
- "Escape to Wisconsin," a large booklet published bi-annually (summer and winter). Includes information on outdoor recreation in the state.
- "Wisconsin Fishing," a foldout that describes fish indigenous to Wisconsin.
- "Wisconsin Auto Tours," a large foldout that features 25 tours in different parts of the state. Includes maps.
- "Wisconsin Public Transportation," a foldout with a map of bus, rail and ferry systems.

Ask for: each publication you want by name
Send: a postcard
To: Wisconsin Dept. of Tourism
Dept. of Development
P.O. Box 7606
Madison, WI 53707

CITIES

Madison

- "Things to See and Do," a foldout about major attractions in the city. Also describes recreation areas.

WISCONSIN

- "Restaurant Guide," a foldout listing more than 60 restaurants, with a map locating them in the city.
- "Hotel/Motel Guide," a foldout describing many accommodations in the area.
- "Madison Brochure," a colorful foldout that includes general information about the city.
- "Calendar of Events," a fact sheet listing many events in the area. Updated twice a year.

Ask for: each publication you want by name
Send: a postcard
To: Greater Madison Convention & Visitors' Bureau
Dept. F
425 W. Washington Ave.
Madison, WI 53703

Milwaukee

Two foldouts about Milwaukee, a city along Lake Michigan. The first publication lists city attractions, parks, museums, sports facilities and more. Provides a large city map. The second foldout is a guide to local happenings, and it's updated every 2 months.

Ask for: "Greater Milwaukee Brochure" and "Calendar of Events"
Send: a postcard

To: Greater Milwaukee Convention & Visitors' Bureau
756 N. Milwaukee St.—FS81
Milwaukee, WI 53202

Whitewater

Two brochures about Whitewater, a town in the southeastern area of Wisconsin. Includes a publication on major attractions, recreation areas and cultural events. Also offers a visitors' guide to the area, highlighting bicycle trails and outdoor recreation activities. Includes several maps.

Ask for: "Whitewater, Wisconsin, Something for Everyone" and "Whitewater Area Visitors' Guide"
Send: a postcard
To: Whitewater Area Chamber of Commerce
P.O. Box 34
Whitewater, WI 53190

PARKS & PUBLIC LANDS

State Parks

A foldout that serves as a guide to all Wisconsin state parks, forests and other recreation lands. Provides a list of facilities, regulations and locations.

Ask for: "State Park Visitor's Guide"
Send: a postcard
To: Wisconsin Dept. of Natural Resources
P.O. Box 7921
Madison, WI 53707

SKI AREAS

Telemark

A one-year subscription (3 issues per ski season) to the *Birch Scroll* newspaper, containing news about cross-country skiing at Telemark, a Wisconsin ski area. Also features details about North America's largest cross-country skiing event, the American Birkebeiner.

Ask for: a subscription to the *Birch Scroll*
Send: a postcard
To: Birch Scroll
Telemark
Dept. F
Cable, WI 54821

ATTRACTIONS

Circus World

A colorful foldout with information about an historical

museum-attraction, Circus World. Describes the many circus acts, demonstrations, animal shows and other displays in this attraction located in southern Wisconsin.

Ask for: "Circus World, Wisconsin's Most Exciting Attraction"
Send: a postcard
To: Circus World Museum
426 Water St.—FST
Baraboo, WI 53913

Sun Prairie

A fact sheet with information from the Sun Prairie Chamber of Commerce about the annual ceremony at the Groundhog Capitol of the World. Includes a description of the groundhog's official winter weather prediction ceremony. Also supplies information about how to secure a Groundhog Birth Certificate, available to anyone with a February 2nd birthday.

Ask for: information on groundhog ceremony
Send: a postcard
To: Chamber of Commerce
243 E. Main St.
Sun Prairie, WI 53590
Attn.: Groundhog

Wyoming

- "Wyoming," a glossy booklet filled with color photographs of state attractions and scenic areas.
- "Wyomingold," a colorful booklet on fall motor tours, attractions and wildlife.
- "Family Water Sports," a foldout about water sports on the state's lakes and streams.
- "Wyoming Events," a calendar of major events and activities. Updated twice a year.

Ask for: each publication you want by name
Send: a postcard
To: Wyoming Travel Commission
Rm. 81—X
Cheyenne, WY 82002

REGIONS

Four large foldouts with information on the 4 regions of Wyoming. Describes recreation areas, historical sites and major events in each of these areas:

- Central
- Southern
- Western
- Northern

Ask for: "Your Self-Guided Tour" (specify 1 or more of the above regions)
Send: a postcard

To: Wyoming Travel Commission
Rm. 81—X
Cheyenne, WY 82002

CITIES

Casper

- "Casper," a small booklet with color photographs of this city in the center of Wyoming.
- "Casper, Local and Area Attractions," a foldout that describes museums and historical and recreational sites.
- "Casper, Accommodations and Restaurants," a foldout listing hotels, motels, campgrounds and restaurants.
- "Casper City Map," a detailed map of the city.
- "Wyoming State Map," an official highway map of the state.

Ask for: each publication you want by name
Send: a postcard
To: Casper Area Chamber of Commerce
P.O. Box 399
Casper, WY 82602
Attn.: Information Secretary

WYOMING

LODGING, CAMPGROUNDS & RESORTS

A comprehensive booklet that lists campgrounds and hotels all over the state and gives the address, rates and facilities of each. Includes campgrounds and lodges in the national parks. Also features a section on dude ranches and resorts.

Ask for: "Big Wyoming Accommodations"
Send: a postcard
To: Wyoming Travel Commission
Rm. 81—X
Cheyenne, WY 82002

PARKS & PUBLIC LANDS

Bureau of Land Management

A foldout that describes the land-user maps available from the Wyoming state office of the U.S. Bureau of Land Management. These maps show historical sites, trails, skiing and snowmobiling areas, campgrounds and more. Includes an index to the available maps and an order form.

Ask for: "Wyoming Public Land User Maps Order Form"
Send: a postcard
To: U.S. Dept. of the Interior
Bureau of Land Management
Wyoming State Office
P.O. Box 1828
Cheyenne, WY 82001

National Parks

- "Yellowstone National Park—Winter," a foldout about winter activities and tours in this national park.
- "Jackson Hole and the Tetons," a colorful booklet of information about the Jackson Hole area. Covers fishing, skiing, horseback riding, sleigh rides and all types of water sports. Includes several sections on activities in Grand Teton National Park.
- "National Parkways—Yellowstone National Park," a booklet that serves as a comprehensive guide to this park, covering scenic sights, walking tours and recreation facilities.

Ask for: each publication you want by name
Send: a postcard

To: Wyoming Travel Commission
Rm. 81—X
Cheyenne, WY 82002

SKI AREAS

A booklet with details on Wyoming's main downhill ski resorts and cross-country ski trails. Also includes information on winter in Yellowstone and Grand Teton National Parks.

Ask for: "Wyoming's Snowtime"
Send: a postcard
To: Wyoming Travel Commission
Rm. 81—X
Cheyenne, WY 82002

HISTORICAL SITES

A foldout that describes historical sites along the route of the old Oregon trail—the route the pioneer wagontrains took through Nebraska and Oregon. Features a number of restored forts.

Ask for: "The Oregon Trail"
Send: a postcard
To: Wyoming Travel Commission
Rm. 81—X
Cheyenne, WY 82002

Washington, D.C.

Five publications to help you plan your visit to the nation's capital.

- "Welcome to Washington," a small map and guide to the major government buildings, museums and galleries in Washington.
- "Washington, D.C.," a full-color pamphlet that lists major attractions, hotels, tour guides, theaters and campgrounds in and around the city.
- "Where to Stay," a brief directory of dozens of

hotels and motels in and around Washington. Includes rates.
- "Guide to Dining," a booklet with capsule descriptions of hundreds of restaurants in Washington.
- "Quarterly Sights & Sounds," a calendar of events.

Ask for: each publication you want by name
Send: a postcard
To: Washington Convention & Visitors' Assn.
Dept. FS–81
1575 Eye St. NW, Ste. 250
Washington, DC 20005

Virgin Islands

- "Things to See & Do: St. Croix," a large foldout with useful information on restaurants, shopping, sightseeing, camping, skin diving, tennis and other activities on the island of St. Croix.
- "Things to See & Do: St. Thomas/St. John," a large foldout with all of the above information for the smaller islands of St. Thomas and St. John.
- "Hotel Rate Sheet," a large foldout with detailed information on the facilities and rates of hotels, apartments,

guest houses and villas on all 3 islands. Includes maps of the islands with the location of accommodations indicated.

Ask for: each publication you want by name
Send: a postcard
To: the office closest to you from the 5 offices listed below

U.S. Virgin Islands
Dept. FS
343 S. Dearborn St.
Chicago, IL 60604

U.S. Virgin Islands
Dept. FS
3450 Wilshire Blvd.
Los Angeles, CA 90010

U.S. Virgin Islands
Dept. FS
100 N. Biscayne Blvd.,
Ste. 1504
Miami, FL 33132

U.S. Virgin Islands
Dept. FS
1270 Ave. of the Americas
Mezzanine
New York, NY 10020

U.S. Virgin Islands
Dept. FS
1050 17th St. NW
Washington, DC 20036

SPECIAL VACATIONS

SPECIAL VACATIONS

CRUISES

Cruising Tips

An illustrated pamphlet from the Cruise Lines International Association that answers common questions about vacations on board a cruise ship. Provides helpful information on the typical costs (including tips), accommodations, food, recreational activities and ship itineraries. Also includes a list of its member cruise lines.

Ask for: "Is Cruising Really for Me?"
Send: a 9" self-addressed, stamped envelope
To: Cruise Lines Intl. Assn.
    Dept. MP
    311 California St.
    San Francisco, CA 94104

Delta Queen

Two full-color booklets describing steamboat cruises along the Mississippi and Ohio rivers. The first booklet features cruises of 2 to 11 days aboard the historic *Delta Queen.* The second describes 3- to 14-night cruises on board the luxury steamboat, the *Mississippi Queen.*

Ask for: *"Delta Queen* Deluxe" and/or *"Mississippi Queen* Deluxe"

Send: 50¢ for each publication
To: Delta Queen Steamboat Co.
    Distribution Dept., Box ST81
    511 Main St.
    Cincinnati, OH 45202

Home Lines

Two illustrated booklets describing deluxe, 7-day cruises from New York to Bermuda and Nassau. The S.S. *Oceanic* visits both islands in a week, while the S.S. *Doric* travels only to Bermuda. Booklets describe facilities on board the 2 ships and include price lists.

Ask for: "S.S. *Oceanic*" and/or "S.S. *Doric*"
Send: a postcard
To: Home Lines Cruises
    Dept. DFS
    1 World Trade Ctr.,
    Ste. 3969
    New York, NY 10048

Prudential Lines

A brief foldout that features 32-day trips across the Atlantic and Mediterranean on cargo ships carrying only 8 passengers. Describes accommodations, meals and activities on board and includes a price list.

Ask for: "A Personal Sea Odyssey"
Send: a postcard
To: Prudential Lines
    Passenger Dept. MC–3
    1 World Trade Ctr.
    New York, NY 10048

Royal Cruise Line

A colorful booklet describing deluxe cruises departing from Los Angeles on the Golden Odyssey. Numerous vacations with a variety of sightseeing stops are available, including the Panama Canal, the Caribbean islands, Portugal, Greece, Morocco and Israel. A list of prices is included.

Ask for: "Golden Odyssey Cruise"
Send: a postcard
To: Royal Cruise Line, Inc.
    1 Maritime Plaza,
    Ste. 660
    San Francisco, CA 94111

Royal Viking Line

A foldout from Royal Viking Line listing many luxury cruises to sites around the world. This Norwegian line offers cruises lasting from 4 to 102 days on your choice of 3 ships.

Ask for: "Royal Viking Line Preview"
Send: a postcard
To: Royal Viking Line
    Dept. K15
    1 Embarcadero Ctr.
    San Francisco, CA 94111

Sailaway Charters

A large packet of information with everything you need to know about Sailaway Yacht

Charter vacations in the Virgin Islands. In addition to the items listed below, you can obtain more specific information if you indicate the number of your party and your estimated dates of travel.

- "Introductory Letter," a guide to the services available from this company, including arrangements for reduced air fare.
- "Charter Recommendation Brochure" and "Yacht Brochure," 2 publications about the yachts available with information on price, departure points and recreational equipment.
- "Welcome Aboard," a foldout with hints on things to bring and tipping practices.
- "Pocket Hints," a foldout informing you about U.S. customs regulations for visitors returning from the Virgin Islands.
- "Sunscreen Rating Form," a fact sheet about sunscreens.
- "Virgin Islands Chart," a large navigational map of the islands and surrounding waters.

Ask for: each publication you want by name
Send: a postcard

To: SailAway Yacht Charter Consultants, Inc.
Dept. FST
3100 N. Lake Shore Dr., Ste. 1013
Chicago, IL 60657

Sitmar Cruises

A colorful booklet from Sitmar Cruises describing many trips available on their 2 spacious ships. Destinations include the Caribbean, South America, Mexico, the Panama Canal, Canada and Alaska. Optional tour packages on land can be added to many of the cruises. Detailed price lists are included.

Ask for: "The Sitmar Experience"
Send: a postcard

To: Sitmar Cruises
1801 S. Hill St.
Los Angeles, CA 90015

SIGHTSEEING TOURS

Amazon Safari Club

A brief, illustrated booklet describing 5 unusual tours of the Amazon jungle offered by the Amazon Safari Club. These tours include trips to cities such as Lima, historical sites like Machu Picchu, and primitive outposts like the Yagua Indian community outside Iquitos. Price list included.

Ask for: "Amazon Safari Club"
Send: a postcard
To: Amazon Safari Club
Dept. FS
P.O. Box 252
Elverson, PA 19520

Aventours

Two colorful booklets from Aventours, an organization that specializes in low-cost camping and motel tours for young adults. The first booklet describes tours of several regions in the United States; the second features trips in Europe, Africa, Asia, Australia, New Zealand, the Caribbean, Canada and South America. Price lists are provided.

SPECIAL VACATIONS

Ask for: "America" and/or "World"
Send: a postcard
To: Aventours Information Ctr.
801 Second Ave.
New York, NY 10017

Cartan Tours

Two full-color booklets describing a variety of escorted tours. The first booklet features 17 vacations to Hawaii; the second offers 12 tours to a variety of locations in Mexico, South and Central America.
Ask for: "Hawaii" and/or "Mexico, South and Central America"
Send: 50¢ for each publication
To: Cartan Tours
Public Relations Dept.
1 Crossroads of Commerce
Rolling Meadows, IL 60008

Club Universe

This travel organization offers a general newsletter and a wide selection of colorful brochures (with price lists) on deluxe vacations in locations all over the world. In order to send for more information, specify the location or locations you are interested in, choosing from the list below. Club Universe will send you a brochure on the specific area or the newsletter, which supplies general information about all the tours.

- Eastern U.S. and Canada
- Western U.S. and Canada
- Hawaii
- Alaska
- Caribbean Cruises
- Bahama Cruises
- Mexico
- South America and Galapagos Islands
- Tahiti and South Pacific
- China, India and Nepal
- Europe
- Israel, Egypt and Greece

Ask for: brochures on the areas you're interested in and/or the newsletter
Send: a postcard
To: Club Universe
Sales Dept.
1671 Wilshire Blvd.
Los Angeles, CA 90017

Marsans International

- "Motorcoach Tours," a booklet that describes escorted motorcoach trips in Spain, Portugal and Morocco.
- "Canary Islands," a foldout on vacations in winter resort apartments and hotels in the Canaries, just off the coast of Africa.
- "Costa del Sol," a foldout on vacations in winter

resort apartments on the south coast of Spain.
- "Mexico," a foldout on tours of Mexico City, Acapulco and more.
- "Spain," a foldout describing vacations in Madrid, Barcelona, Seville, Granada, Cordoba and the Costa del Sol.
- "World Cup Soccer Championship," materials on the 1982 championship to be held in Spain during June and July.
- "Rio, Argentina and Peru," a foldout on 3 vacations in South American cities such as Rio de Janeiro, Buenos Aires and Lima.

Ask for: each publication you want by name
Send: a postcard
To: Marsans Intl.
500 Fifth Ave.
New York, NY 10010

Olson-Travelworld

An extensive pamphlet listing escorted tours to Africa, China, the Soviet Union, Europe, India, the Middle East, South America and the South Pacific.
Ask for: "World Wide Vacation Guide"
Send: a postcard

To: Olson-Travelworld Ltd.
P.O. Box 92734
Los Angeles, CA 90009

Thomson Vacations

A comprehensive booklet (with price list) on "winter sun" vacations in the Bahamas, the Caribbean and Mexico. An added feature is the Junior Vacation Club, a group of hotels that offer facilities and services for families with young children. Along with the vacation booklet, this company will send a sturdy luggage tag with removable address labels.
Ask for: "Winter Sun Vacations" and "Luggage Tag"
Send: 50¢
To: Thomson Vacations, Inc.
401 N. Michigan Ave.,
Ste. 2900
Chicago, IL 60611

Westours

- "Alaska Cruises and Tours," a detailed booklet offering many types of Alaskan vacations, by sea, land and air.
- "Canadian Rockies," a colorful booklet of fully escorted motorcoach tours to scenic areas like Lake Louise, Jasper, Glacier and Yellowstone National Parks, and Banff.

- "West," a booklet describing motorcoach tours throughout Arizona, Utah, Nevada, California, Oregon, Washington and the Canadian Rockies.

Ask for: each publication you want by name
Send: a postcard
To: Westours, Inc.
300 Elliott Ave. W
Seattle, WA 98119

ORGANIZED EXPEDITIONS

Bikecentennial

A large catalog about cycling tours and publications offered by this nonprofit organization for bicyclists. Lists organized tours all over the country plus available maps, guidebooks and how-to books on cycling all over the world.
Ask for: "Bike Back Into America"
Send: $1.00
To: Bikecentennial
P.O. Box 8308T
Missoula, MT 59807

Brad's Tours

A complete schedule of hiking, ski-touring, birdwatching and naturalist tours in Hawaii, Alaska, Texas, Washington and British Columbia. Also contains detailed information on the trip ac-

tivities. Offer includes 4 mailings of this material.
Ask for: tour schedule and information
Send: $1.00 (for 4 mailings)
To: Brad's Tours
Dept. MP
9112 284th St. NE
Arlington, WA 98223

Grand Canyon Youth Expeditions

A schedule of rafting and hiking trips in the Grand Canyon area. Trips are designed for 2 levels: "family" or "youth" (6- to 15-year-olds). Also provides general information.
Ask for: "Grand Canyon Youth Expeditions"
Send: a 9" self-addressed envelope with 2 first-class stamps attached
To: Grand Canyon Youth Expeditions
R. Rte. 4, Box 755
Flagstaff, AZ 86001

Lankford Mountain Guides

A large foldout describing backpacking, ski-touring and mountaineering trips in Colorado, Montana, Wyoming, Alaska, Mexico, Switzerland and Africa. Trips are offered at beginner, intermediate and advanced levels, and many provide instruction.

SPECIAL VACATIONS

Ask for: "Lankford Mountain Guides"
Send: a postcard
To: Lankford Mountain Guides
333 Fairfax St.
Denver, CO 80220

Liberty Bell Alpine

A foldout that features backpacking, climbing, ski-touring, bicycling, white-water rafting and kayaking tours in the Cascade Mountains in Washington. Trips range in ability from beginner to advanced.
Ask for: "Liberty Bell Alpine Tours"
Send: a postcard
To: Liberty Bell Alpine Tours
Star Rte. #1
Mazama, WA 98833

Mid-America River Voyageurs

A large booklet that lists canoeing, hiking and ski-touring trips offered year round in all parts of the country. Trips range in ability from beginner to intermediate including several family-oriented trips. Also describes several backpacking and mountaineering courses.
Ask for: "MARV"
Send: a postcard
To: MARV
P.O. Box 125
Spencer, IA 51301

O.A.R.S./Sobek

A colorful catalog featuring white-water canoe trips throughout the United States. Also describes rafting, mountaineering, horseback riding, sailing and climbing tours all over the world (including South America, Africa, Nepal and New Guinea). Trips range from beginning to extremely advanced levels.
Ask for: "O.A.R.S./Sobek Catalog"
Send: a postcard
To: O.A.R.S./Sobek River Trips
P.O. Box 67FS
Angels Camp, CA 95222

Old West Tours

A publication that describes motorcoach, river rafting, dude ranching, horsepacking and cross-country skiing vacations in Yellowstone and Grand Teton National Parks. All tours are moderately paced and suitable for individuals, families and groups.
Ask for: "Old West Tours"
Send: $1.00
To: Brochure
Old West Tours
P.O. Box 371
Jackson, WY 83001

Riverrun North

Large 17" x 11" maps of the Housatonic and Farmington Rivers in Massachusetts and Connecticut that mark recommended canoeing routes, campsites and access points.
Ask for: map of Housatonic and/or Farmington Rivers
Send: a postcard
To: Riverrun North
P.O. Box 636F
Sheffield, MA 01257

Saco Bound

A full-color foldout that describes raft trips in New Hampshire and Maine as well as the courses offered by the Northern Waters Whitewater School. Also includes information on renting equipment.

Ask for: "Saco Bound Northern Waters"
Send: a postcard
To: Saco Bound
P.O. Box 113
Center Conway, NH 03813

Sundance Expeditions

A full-color booklet with information on Sundance kayak and river rafting schools, expeditions in Oregon and California, and steelhead fishing trips. Also includes a foldout on sailing charters in the Baja in Mexico.

Ask for: "Sundance Expeditions" and/or "Baja Sea Ventures"
Send: a postcard
To: Sundance Expeditions, Inc.
14894 Galice Rd.
Merlen, OR 97532

Sunrise County Canoe Expeditions

A pamphlet with information on the services offered by this guide and outfitting company. Although they specialize in guiding private adult and family groups, they also offer a number of scheduled canoe trips each year in Maine and Labrador, as well as a youth wilderness canoe program.

Ask for: "Sunrise County Canoe Expeditions"
Send: a postcard

To: Sunrise County Canoe Expeditions, Inc.
Cathance Lake
Grove P.O., ME 04638

Trailhead Ventures

A schedule of backpacking trips in the central Colorado Rockies. Trips include a beginner backpacking expedition, a peak climbing week, a photography workshop and an all-woman backpacking group. Also features a brochure on the company and its guides.

Ask for: "Trip Schedule" and/or "Trailhead Ventures"
Send: a postcard
To: The Trailhead
Dept. FS
P.O. Box CC
Buena Vista, CO 81211

University of the Wilderness

A newsletter that describes University of the Wilderness activities, such as nature-study field trips and ski-touring, canoeing and hiking trips all over the country. Also gives information on the Wilderness Sojourners, a wilderness trip cooperative.

Ask for: "University of the Wilderness Catalog"
Send: 50¢
To: University of the Wilderness
P.O. Box 1687
Evergreen, CO 80439

Wilderness River Outfitters

A colorful booklet that describes rafting, backpacking and ski-touring trips in Montana, Idaho, Oregon and Alaska. Most trips require good physical condition and some previous experience.

Ask for: "Wilderness River Outfitters"
Send: a postcard
To: Wilderness River Outfitters
P.O. Box 871F
Salmon, ID 83467

Wilderness Southeast

A large booklet that describes this school of the outdoors and the programs it offers. The school's trips include canoeing in the Okefenokee Swamp of Georgia and the Everglades of Florida, sailing and snorkeling along the southern coast, and backpacking in the Smoky Mountains. Also offers photography workshops and classes in wild food foraging.

Ask for: "Program Catalog"
Send: $1.00
To: Wilderness Southeast, Inc.
9521–FS Whitfield Ave.
Savannah, GA 31406

Wildwater, Ltd.

Two foldouts describing the outfitting services, guided

SPECIAL VACATIONS

rafting trips, and canoe and kayak clinics offered by Wildwater, Ltd. All trips and clinics take place on the Chattooga, Hiwassee, Ocoee and Nolichucky rivers in South Carolina and Tennessee.

Ask for: "Tennessee Whitewater" and "Chattooga River Rafting"
Send: a 9" self-addressed, stamped envelope
To: Wildwater, Ltd.
    Outdoor Adventures
    Long Creek, SC 29658

EQUIPMENT

A number of catalogs of camping and hiking equipment are available from mail-order companies around the country. If the catalog is free, just send a postcard.

Ask for: "Outdoor Catalog" (free)
    Eddie Bauer
    Dept. AJ3
    Fifth and Union
    Seattle, WA 98124

Ask for: current catalog (free)
    L. L. Bean, Inc.
    9980 Spruce St.
    Freeport, ME 04033

Ask for: current catalog (free)
    Camping World
    Dept. Spa
    Beech Bend Rd.
    Bowling Green, KY 42101

Ask for: current catalog (free)
    Campmor
    P.O. Box 407MP
    Bogota, NJ 07603

Ask for: current catalog (free)
    The Cannondale Corp.
    35 Pulaskie St.
    Stamford, CT 06902

Ask for: "Kits from Country Ways" (free)
    Country Ways, Inc.
    3500 S. Hwy. 101
    Minnetonka, MN 55343

Ask for: current catalog (free)
    Early Winters, Ltd.
    110–PH Prefontaine Pl. S
    Seattle, WA 98104

Ask for: "Eureka! Tent Catalog" (50¢) and/or "Camp Trails Catalog" (50¢)
    Johnson Camping, Inc.
    Marketing Asst.
    P.O. Box 966
    Binghamton, NY 13903

Ask for: current catalog (free)
    R.E.I. Co-op
    P.O. Box C–88125
    Seattle, WA 98188

HOTELS & MOTELS

Directories of hotel and motel chains around the country are described below. Using double occupancy rates (2 persons, 1 bed) as our base, we've identified the price ranges you're likely to find in **most** of the member hotels or motels. At certain locations, however, you may find higher or lower prices.

$	(Inexpensive)	$19–$25
$$	(Moderate)	$25–$45
$$$	(Expensive)	$45 and up

Bed & Breakfast International $$

Three foldouts from an organization that arranges reservations for lodgings in private homes in several western states, New York City, Hawaii and England. Policies include a 3-night minimum stay in major cities and a required $15 deposit when making reservations. A full breakfast is included in the price, and occasional use of kitchen and laundry facilities is allowed.
Ask for: information on Bed & Breakfast International

Send: a 9" self-addressed envelope with 2 first-class stamps attached
To: Bed & Breakfast Intl.
151 Ardmore Rd.
Kensington, CA 94707

Best Value Inns $–$$

A pamphlet listing hundreds of member inns located throughout the United States. Includes addresses, phone numbers, rates and a description of the facilities. Also provides a small reservation form and 4 "save-a-dollar coupons."
Ask for: "Best Value Inns Member Directory"
Send: a postcard
To: Best Value Inn
Directory Service
1115 E. Hennepin Ave.
Minneapolis, MN 55414

Best Western International $$

A colorful booklet from Best Western International, listing hundreds of hotels and motels in the United States, Canada and Mexico. Offers many full-color road maps, in addition to detailed directions to each hotel or motel. Addresses, phone numbers, facilities, nearby activities and rates are also provided.

Ask for: "Best Western Road Atlas and Travel Guide"
Send: 75¢
To: Best Western Intl.
Travel Guide Request
P.O. Box 10203
Phoenix, AZ 85064

Budget Host Inns $

A pamphlet listing more than 100 inns across the United States and Canada. Provides addresses, phone numbers, rates and a description of the facilities. Includes a map of the United States locating each inn.
Ask for: "Budget Host Travel Directory"
Send: a 9" self-addressed, stamped envelope
To: Budget Host
Travel Directory
Dept. FS
P.O. Box 10656
Fort Worth, TX 76114

Downtowner-Passport Inns $$

A booklet of information about dozens of inns located throughout the United States. Includes addresses, phone numbers and current rates. Also describes nearby attractions. Several regional maps are included.
Ask for: "Downtowner-Passport Inn Directory"

HOTELS & MOTELS

Send: a postcard
To: Downtowner-Passport
System
5350 Poplar Ave., Ste. 518
P.O. Box 171807
Memphis, TN 38119

Econo-Travel Motor Hotels $

A pamphlet of information about over 100 budget motor hotels and lodges across the United States and Canada. These motels are designed to be the most economical accommodations possible, without frills such as pools, restaurants and banquet halls. The directory provides addresses, phone numbers, facilities and rates. Regional maps are also included.

Ask for: "Econo-Travel Motor Hotels Directory"
Send: a postcard
To: Econo-Travel Motor
Hotel Corp.
Directory Request—MP
P.O. Box 12188
Norfolk, VA 23502

Friendship Inns $–$$

A packet of information on over 1000 inns located in the United States, Canada, Mexico, Germany and Japan. Includes a travel guide with full addresses, phone numbers and rates for the inns, a fold-out with tips on saving gas and a discount card worth a $1.00 discount on a room for 2 persons or more.

Ask for: "Travel Guide" and "Gas Questions"
Send: $1.00
To: Friendship Inns Intl.
739 S. 400th St. W
Salt Lake City, UT 84101

Howard Johnson's $$

A comprehensive directory of hundreds of motor lodges across the United States and Canada. Features a detailed listing for each hotel, including a street map, address, phone number, rates and a guide to nearby attractions. Also provides a list of Howard Johnson's restaurants.

Ask for: "Motor Lodge Directory"
Send: a postcard
To: Howard Johnson Co.
Marketing Dept.
222 Forbes Rd.
Braintree, MA 02188
Attn.: Motor Lodge
Directories

Inter-Continental Hotels $$$

A pamphlet listing more than 80 deluxe hotels in locations all over the world, including Europe, Africa, the Middle East, Asia, Latin America, the United States and Canada. Provides descriptions of the hotels with addresses and phone numbers. A price list is not included.

Ask for: "Inter-Continental Hotel Directory"
Send: a postcard
To: Inter-Continental Hotels
Marketing Dept.
Pan Am Bldg., Rm. 436W
New York, NY 10166

La Quinta Motor Inns $$

A pamphlet of information about dozens of motor inns across the southern half of the United States. Includes addresses, phone numbers, nearby attractions, facilities and rates. Provides street maps of the area surrounding each inn.

Ask for: "La Quinta Directory"
Send: a postcard
To: La Quinta Marketing
Dept. FS
4100 McEwen, Ste. 283
Dallas, TX 75234

Magic Key Inns $$

A list of dozens of member inns across the country. Offers the address and phone number for each inn. Also includes a card that can be

redeemed for a $6.00 refund when you stay at a member inn for at least 6 nights.
Ask for: "Magic Key Inns" member list
Send: a postcard
To: Magic Key Inns of America
P.O. Box 1667
Yakima, WA 98907

Marriott Hotels $$$

A booklet describing dozens of deluxe hotels in the United States, Europe, Central America, Mexico, the Caribbean and the Middle East. Provides a description of the facilities and nearby attractions for each hotel. Also lists addresses, phone numbers and rates.
Ask for: "Marriott Hotels Directory"
Send: a postcard
To: Marriott Hotels
Dept. 873–11
Marriott Dr.
Washington, DC 20058

Motel 6, Inc. $

A pamphlet listing over 100 budget motels across the United States. Includes phone numbers, addresses, directions, nearby attractions and street maps. Rates are the same at all motels.
Ask for: "Motel 6 Directory"

Send: a 9" self-addressed, stamped envelope
To: Motel 6, Inc.
Dept. M
51 Hitchcock Way
Santa Barbara, CA 93105

Quality Inns, International $$

A pamphlet from Quality Inns, International that lists over 350 inns in the United States, Canada and Mexico. Provides the phone number, address, nearby attractions, street map and rates for each inn. Also includes a list of mini-vacation packages.
Ask for: "Travel Directory"
Send: a postcard
To: Travel Directory
Dept. TD
P.O. Box 767
Silver Spring, MD 20901

Ramada Inns $$

A colorful booklet describing hundreds of inns in the United States, Canada, Mexico, Europe, Asia, Australia and the Middle East. Includes full address, phone number, list of attractions, street map and rates for each inn.
Ask for: "Ramada Inn Directory"
Send: a postcard

To: Ramada Inn
P.O. Box 590MP
Phoenix, AZ 85001

Red Roof Inns $

A fact sheet on dozens of motels located mainly in the midwestern and eastern states. Lists the address and phone number for each inn. Also provides a chart of rates and typical facilities available.
Ask for: "Red Roof Inns Directory"
Send: a postcard
To: Red Roof Inns, Inc.
Dept. FST
4355 Davidson Rd.
Amlin, OH 43002

Super 8 Motels $

A colorful pamphlet about this chain of about 100 motels located throughout the United States. Describes the facilities and nearby attractions for each motel. Also lists the address, phone number and rates.
Ask for: "Super 8 National Directory"
Send: a postcard
To: Super 8 Motels, Inc.
P.O. Box 1456
Aberdeen, SD 57401

FOREIGN COUNTRIES

FOREIGN COUNTRIES

Aruba

A colorful booklet filled with information about Aruba, an island in the Caribbean only 15 miles north of South America. This small island offers white beaches, rolling hills and historic gold mill ruins. Listings of major attractions, hotels, restaurants, water sports, evening activities, local customs and an annual calendar of events are provided in this booklet, which also includes a detailed map of the island.

Ask for: "Aruba Bonbini"
Send: a postcard
To: Aruba Tourist Bureau
Dept. ABB
1270 Ave. of the Americas
New York, NY 10020

Canada

In addition to the more general introductory publications listed below, the Canadian Government Office of Tourism provides a wealth of information on accommodations, attractions, special events and recreation oppor-

tunities for specific areas all over the country.

- "Canada Travel Information," a pamphlet for visitors from the U.S. that deals with entry into Canada, vehicles and motoring, customs regulations, weather, holidays and shopping.
- "Canada Highway Map," a planning map that shows all parts of Canada accessible by road and the highway entry routes from the U.S.
- "Touring Canada," a comprehensive booklet with 56 auto tours designed to take in major attractions and events across Canada.

Ask for: each publication you want by name and/or information on regions you are interested in
Send: a postcard
To: Canadian Government Office of Tourism
235 Queen St.
Ottawa, Ontario
Canada K1A OH6

Denmark

- "General Travel Information," a large foldout with a map of Denmark, information on transportation

to and in Denmark, customs and entry formalities, climate, and bank and shopping hours.
- "Denmark," a full-color booklet describing hotels; restaurants; and shopping, sightseeing and cultural activities in Copenhagen and the provinces.
- "Copenhagen and North Sealand," a booklet with extensive information on museums, attractions, festivals, stores, restaurants, hotels and campgrounds in the capital of Denmark and the surrounding area.
- "Active Holidays," a full-color booklet that features bicycling, golf, tennis, sailing, hiking, canoeing and other active holidays that you can arrange on your own or do as part of an organized tour.

Ask for: each publication you want by name
Send: a postcard
To: Danish Tourist Board
75 Rockefeller Plaza
New York, NY 10019

Egypt

An informative foldout for visitors to Egypt. Includes descriptions of customs regulations, transportation schedules, climate and Arabic vocabulary. Also features a small map.

Ask for: "Travel Information on Egypt"
Send: a 9" self-addressed, stamped envelope
To: Egyptian Government Tourist Office
Dept. FS
630 Fifth Ave.
New York, NY 10020

France

A packet of information on travel to the many unique regions of France. These brochures may supply general traveling tips or specific information on accommodations, restaurants, attractions and historical sites.

Ask for: tourist information on France and its regions
Send: a postcard
To: French Government Tourist Office
610 Fifth Ave.
New York, NY 10960

Paris

Two foldouts with useful information on Paris. The first suggests 7 walking tours around the city and its environs. Highlights of the tours include museums, historical sites, gardens, cathedrals, theaters and cafes. A brief street map is also provided. The second foldout lists dozens of inexpensive restaurants in the Paris area, most of them located near popular monuments. It describes each restaurant's address, phone number, menu, hours and prices. Essential vocabulary terms and a street map are also included.

Ask for: "Paris a Pied" and "Inexpensive Paris Restaurants"
Send: a 9" self-addressed envelope with 2 first-class stamps attached
To: Air France
P.O. Box 10-747
Long Island City, NY 11101

Germany

A large, full-color foldout about the Federal Republic of Germany and West Berlin. In addition to many photographs of the area, it discusses geography, climate, culture, accommodations, transportation and camping facilities. A detailed highway map is also provided.

Ask for: "Welcome to Germany"
Send: a postcard

To: German National Tourist Office
630 Fifth Ave.
New York, NY 10111

Indonesia

A packet of materials for tourists interested in Indonesia, a nation of more than 13,000 islands in southeast Asia, north of Australia. Includes a travel planning guide, a variety of maps, a foldout describing artistic and cultural attractions, a list of accommodations, a calendar of events and a timetable for Garuda Airways, the major national air service.

Ask for: tourist information on Indonesia
Send: a postcard
To: Indonesian Tourist Promotion Office
323 Geary St., Ste. 305
San Francisco, CA 94102

Ireland

Two publications for travelers to Ireland. A detailed pamphlet that covers accommodations, transportation, outdoor activities, attractions, museums, historical sites, motor tours, a calendar of events and a list of tourist information offices. Also a colorful booklet filled with photographs and facts about Ireland. Includes a large map.

Ask for: "Traveler's Guide" and "From Ireland With Love"
Send: a postcard
To: Irish Tourist Board
Dept. SK–1
590 Fifth Ave.
New York, NY 10036

Israel

- "Visitor's Companion," an extensive booklet that supplies general data about traveling to the country, accommodations, entertainment and sightseeing.
- "Israel Touring Map" shows youth hostels, local tourist information offices, campsites, national parks, historical sites and kibbutz inns.
- "Israel on Your Own" has 16 regional maps plus a table of distances.
- "Calendar of Events," a large booklet detailing month-to-month activities all over the country.

- "Tourist Hotels," a large booklet that lists graded hotels city by city and gives information on rates.
- "Camping," a foldout listing campsites and describing facilities.
- "Kibbutz Inns," a full-color booklet, lists 20 guest houses on working communities that are open to visitors.
- "Shopping, Cafes and Restaurants Guide" gives tips on clothing sizes, shopping hours and transportation.

Ask for: each publication you want by name
Send: a postcard
To: the regional office serving your state.

Residents of CT, DE, DC, ME, MD, MA, NH, NJ, NY, PA, RI, VA, VT, WV should contact:
Israel Government Tourist Office
350 Fifth Ave.
New York, NY 10001

Residents of IL, IA, IN, KS, KY, MI, MN, MO, NE, ND, OH, SD, WI should contact:
Israel Government Tourist Office
5 S. Wabash Ave.
Chicago, IL 60603

Residents of AK, AZ, CA, CO, HI, ID, MT, NM, NV, OR, UT, WA, WY should contact:
Israel Government Tourist Office
6380 Wilshire Blvd.
Los Angeles, CA 90048

Residents of AL, AR, FL, GA, LA, MS, NC, OK, SC, TN, TX should contact:
Israel Government Tourist Office
795 Peachtree St. NE
Atlanta, GA 30308

Mexico

An illustrated booklet describing Mexico's major cities—Acapulco, Guadalajara, La Paz, Mazatlan, Mexico City and others. Lists attractions, outdoor activities and historical sites in these cities. Also provides a route map for Aeromexico airline.

Ask for: "Aeromexico's Great Cities"
Send: a postcard
To: Aeromexico Tour Distribution Ctr.
Dept. FST–81
3322 La Cienega Pl.
Los Angeles, CA 90016

St. Maarten

A colorful foldout about this island in the Netherland Antilles in the Caribbean. Provides a brief summary of the island's attractions. Also available is an issue of a monthly guide to vacation activities and shopping bargains on the island. Includes many tips on good buys in Philipsburg, St. Maarten's capital.

Ask for: "St. Maarten" and "St. Maarten Holiday"
Send: a postcard
To: St. Maarten Tourist Office
Dept. FSFT
445 Park Ave., Ste. 903
New York, NY 10022

Senegal

A packet of assorted brochures on Senegal, a country on the western coast of Africa. Includes information on accommodations, entertainment, historical sites, tours, safaris, game parks and nature reserves.

Ask for: tourist information on Senegal
Send: a postcard

To: Senegal Tourist Bureau
200 Park Ave., East Lobby
New York, NY 10017

Singapore

Three publications about Singapore, a city on an island south of Malaysia.

- "Welcome to Singapore," a comprehensive booklet introducing you to Singapore and its history, climate, shopping bargains, entertainment, restaurants and sights. Includes detailed information on hotels and transportation to and in Singapore.
- "Singapore Insights," a booklet describing the major attractions in the city. Suggests 4 tours designed to take in most of these sightseeing "musts."
- "The Singapore Handicraft Centre," a foldout on this center for Asian arts and crafts.

Ask for: each publication you want by name
Send: a postcard
To: Singapore Tourist
Promotion Board
342 Madison Ave., Rm. 1008
New York, NY 10173

Spain

- "Spain," a large booklet offering a general introduction to Spain's history, museums, recreational opportunities, shopping and festivals. Includes many full-color photographs.
- "General Information," a foldout that gives general tips on travel to Spain.
- "Spain—Communications Routes," a roadmap of Spain with inserts of the major cities.

Ask for: each publication you want by name
Send: a postcard
To: Pilar Vico
Spanish National Tourist Office
665 Fifth Ave.
New York, NY 10022

Switzerland

- "Travel Tips for Switzerland," a pamphlet with general information on accommodations, outdoor recreation, transportation, youth travel and some general Swiss customs and practices.

FOREIGN COUNTRIES

- "Unique World of Switzerland," a very readable booklet describing each of Switzerland's 14 regions. Suggests sightseeing walks or mountain hikes in each area and lists some recommended local inns.
- "Swiss Holiday Card," a foldout with a map of Switzerland and information on travel by train, lake steamer and bus.
- "Switzerland," a large booklet with full-color photographs of the 14 regions of Switzerland and information on the history, culture and people.

Ask for: each publication you want by name
Send: a postcard
To: Swiss National
    Tourist Office
    The Swiss Ctr.
    608 Fifth Ave.
    New York, NY 10020

Thailand

A packet of assorted publications on Thailand, a country in the southeast corner of Asia. Generally includes a fact sheet, a calendar of events, a list of attractions, several foldouts on specific sites, a guide to accommodations and several maps. Features many tips for planning a visit to Bangkok, the nation's capital.

Ask for: tourist information on Thailand
Send: a postcard
To: Tourism Authority of
    Thailand
    5 World Trade Ctr., Ste. 2449
    New York, NY 10048

Yugoslavia

The Yugoslav National Tourist Office offers many publications on the Yugoslav Federal Republic, cities and resorts. Listed below are those publications that cover the whole country—however, if you are planning to visit a particular city or region, indicate this and you will receive more detailed information on the area specified.

- "Yugoslavia," a booklet introducing you to the history, culture and people of Yugoslavia. Includes many full-color photographs.
- "Yugoslavia Travel Guide" gives general facts on major cities and resorts, along with more detailed information on sightseeing tours, accommodations and travel by ferry, rail and bus.
- "Yugoslavia—Tourist Map," a large foldout with a map of the entire country and 8 suggested tours.
- "Yugoslavia—Sunny Adriatic," a large booklet with a detailed map of the Adriatic coast and descriptions of all the resorts and their facilities.
- "Yugoslavia National Parks," a large booklet, lists recreational opportunities in the parks, mountains, rivers and lakes of Yugoslavia.

Ask for: each publication you want by name and/or information on specific cities or regions
Send: a postcard
To: Yugoslav National
    Tourist Office
    630 Fifth Ave.
    New York, NY 10111

Place Index

Foreign continents, countries and areas

Africa, 101–104
Aruba, 112
Asia, 101
Australia, 101
Bahamas, 102–103
Bermuda, 100
Canada, 10, 101–103, 105, 112
Caribbean, 24, 101–103
Central America, 101–102
China, 102
Denmark, 112
Egypt, 102, 112–113
England, 10
Europe, 101–102
France, 113
Germany, 113
Greece, 102
India, 102
Indonesia, 113
Ireland, 10, 113–114
Israel, 114
Mexico, 101–103, 105, 114
Morocco, 102
Nassau, 100
Nepal, 102, 104
New Guinea, 104
New Zealand, 101
Portugal, 102
St. Maarten, 115
Senegal, 115
Singapore, 115
South America, 101–102, 104
Soviet Union, 102
Spain, 102, 115
Switzerland, 103, 115–116
Thailand, 116
Yugoslavia, 116
United States and territories
Alabama, 26–27

Alaska, 27–28, 101–103, 105
Arizona, 28–29, 103
Arkansas, 29
California, 29–34, 103, 105
Colorado, 35–36, 105
Connecticut, 35–36, 104
Delaware, 36–37
District of Columbia. *See* Washington, D.C.
Florida, 37–39, 105
Georgia, 39–41, 105
Hawaii, 41–42, 102–103
Idaho, 42–43, 105
Illinois, 43–45
Indiana, 45–46
Iowa, 46–48
Kansas, 48
Kentucky, 48–50
Louisiana, 50–51
Maine, 51–52, 104–105
Maryland, 52–53
Massachusetts, 53–55, 104
Michigan, 55–57
Minnesota, 57–59
Mississippi, 59–61
Missouri, 61–62
Montana, 62–63, 103, 105
Nebraska, 63–64
Nevada, 64–65, 103
New Hampshire, 65, 104
New Jersey, 65
New Mexico, 66–67
New York, 67–72
North Carolina, 72–74
North Dakota, 74
Ohio, 74–76
Oklahoma, 76–77
Oregon, 77–78, 103, 105
Pennsylvania, 78–81
Rhode Island, 81–82
South Carolina, 82, 106
South Dakota, 82–83
Tennessee, 84–85, 106
Texas, 86–88, 103

Utah, 88–89
Vermont, 89–90
Virginia, 90–92
Virgin Islands, 97, 101
Washington, 92–93, 103–104
Washington, D.C., 97
West Virginia, 93
Wisconsin, 93–95
Wyoming, 95–96, 103

Subject Index

Accidents, automobile, 9. *See also* Auto travel; Emergencies, medical
Airline travel, 20
Attractions (such as amusement parks, aquaria, halls of fame, zoos)
—in foreign countries: Aruba, 112; Denmark, 112; France, 113; Ireland, 113; Israel, 114; Mexico, 114; St. Maarten, 115; Senegal, 115; Singapore, 115; Spain, 115; Thailand, 116
—in the U.S.: Ala., 26–27; Alaska, 27; Ariz., 28; Ark., 29; Calif., 30–33; Colo., 34; Conn., 35–36; D.C., 97; Fla., 37–39; Ga., 39–40; Ill., 43–44; Ind., 46; Iowa, 46–47; Kans., 48; Ky., 49; Mass., 55; Mich., 56; Minn., 57–59; Mo., 61; Nebr., 63; Nev., 64; N.J., 65; N.Mex., 66; N.Y., 67–69, 71; N.C., 72–73; N.Dak., 74; Ohio, 74–76; Okla., 76; Oreg., 77; Pa., 81; Tenn., 85; Tex., 86–88; Vt., 89; Va., 91; Wash., 92; W.Va., 93; Wis., 94–95
Auto travel: accidents, 8; conserving gas, 6–7; emergencies, 9; repairs, 7–8;

INDEX

INDEX

Your Organization Can Be in the Next Edition!

To be considered for the next edition, please send us samples of the travel materials you would like to offer, with a letter expressing your interest. There is no charge for a listing, but you must be willing to respond to single–copy requests through the pledge date.

Send your materials to:
Meadowbrook Press
Dept. FST83
18318 Minnetonka Blvd.
Deephaven, MN 55391

FREE STUFF BOOKS

FREE STUFF FOR KIDS
Over 250 of the best free and up-to-a-dollar things kids can get by mail:
- coins & stamps
- bumper stickers & decals
- posters & maps

$3.70 ppd.

FREE STUFF FOR COOKS
Over 250 of the best free and up-to-a-dollar booklets and samples cooks can get by mail:
- cookbooks & recipe cards
- money-saving shopping guides
- seeds & spices

$3.70 ppd.

FREE STUFF FOR PARENTS
Over 250 of the best free and up-to-a-dollar booklets and samples parents can get by mail:
- sample teethers
- booklets on pregnancy & childbirth
- sample newsletters

$3.70 ppd.

FREE STUFF FOR HOME & GARDEN
Over 350 of the best free and up-to-a-dollar booklets and samples homeowners and gardeners can get by mail:
- booklets on home improvement & energy
- plans for do-it-yourself projects
- sample seeds

$3.70 ppd.

FREE STUFF FOR TRAVELERS
Over 1000 of the best free and up-to-a-dollar publications and products travelers can get by mail:
- guidebooks to cities, states & foreign countries
- pamphlets on attractions, festivals & parks
- posters, calendars & maps

$3.70 ppd.

THE BEST BABY NAME BOOK
The most complete, up-to-date, helpful, entertaining and gifty baby name book ever. Includes over 10,000 names. Introduction by Erma Bombeck.

$3.70 ppd.

THE BEST FREE ATTRACTIONS

THE BEST FREE ATTRACTIONS

THE BEST FREE ATTRACTIONS SOUTH

From North Carolina to Texas, it's a land swarming with surprises – and over 1,500 of them free:
- alligator and turtle stalking
- cow chip tosses & mule races
- free bluegrass, watermelon & barbecues!

THE BEST FREE ATTRACTIONS WEST

Just passing through from California to Montana? It's all free and there for the asking:
- belching volcanoes & miniature forests
- gold panning & quarter horse racing
- vineyard tours and free wine samples!

THE BEST FREE ATTRACTIONS EAST

Over 1,500 irresistible attractions – all free – from West Virginia to Maine (the proper east coast):
- a witchtrial courthouse with evidence
- aviaries where *you* are caged
- the "gentle giants" – and free beer!

THE BEST FREE ATTRACTIONS MIDWEST

From Kentucky to North Dakota, the Midwest is chock-full of free things:
- camel rides and shark feedings
- stagecoaches and magic tricks
- hobo conventions – with free Mulligan stew!

SOUTH

Alabama, Arkansas, Florida, Georgia, Louisiana, Mississippi, North Carolina, Oklahoma, South Carolina, Tennessee, Texas

WEST

Alaska, Arizona, California, Colorado, Hawaii, Idaho, Montana, Nevada, New Mexico, Oregon, Utah, Washington, Wyoming

EAST

Connecticut, Delaware, DC, Maine, Maryland, Massachusetts, New Hampshire, New Jersey, New York, Pennsylvania, Rhode Island, Vermont, Virginia, West Virginia

MIDWEST

Illinois, Indiana, Iowa, Kansas, Kentucky, Michigan, Minnesota, Missouri, Nebraska, North Dakota, Ohio, South Dakota, Wisconsin

$4.70 ppd. each

BOOKS BY VICKI LANSKY

Hundreds of parent-tested ideas for the first five years. Includes topics such as baby care, feeding, self esteem and more. **Spiral bound. $4.70 ppd.**

The most popular baby book and tot food cookbook for new parents. Includes over 200 recipes and ideas. **Spiral bound. $4.70 ppd.**

The classic cookbook that helps you get your children to eat less sugary, salty junk food . . . and like it! **Spiral bound. $4.70 ppd.**